Answer Set Programming

Vladimir Lifschitz

Answer Set Programming

 Springer

Vladimir Lifschitz
Department of Computer Science
University of Texas at Austin
Austin, TX, USA

ISBN 978-3-030-24657-0   ISBN 978-3-030-24658-7   (eBook)
https://doi.org/10.1007/978-3-030-24658-7

This Springer imprint is published by the registered company Springer Nature Switzerland AG.
The registered company address is: Gewerbestrasse 11, 6330 Cham, Switzerland

To the community of computer scientists, mathematicians, and philosophers who invented answer set programming and are working hard to make it better

"What constitutes the dignity of a craft is that it creates a fellowship, that it binds men together and fashions for them a common language."
                                        – Antoine de Saint-Exupéry

Preface

Answer set programming is a programming methodology rooted in research on artificial intelligence and computational logic. It was created at the turn of the century, and it is now used in many areas of science and technology.

This book is about the art of programming for CLINGO—one of the most efficient and widely used answer set programming systems available today—and about the mathematics of answer set programming. It is based on an undergraduate class taught at the University of Texas at Austin. The book is self-contained; the only prerequisite is some familiarity with programming and discrete mathematics.

Chapter 1 describes the main ideas of answer set programming and its place in the world of programming languages. Chapter 2 explains, in an informal way, several constructs available in the input language of CLINGO. Chapter 3 shows how they can be used to solve a number of computational problems. Chapters 4–6 put the discussion of answer set programming on a firm mathematical foundation. (Reading Chap. 6 is not necessary for understanding the rest of the book.) Chapter 7 describes a few more programming constructs and gives examples of their use. In Chap. 8, answer set programming is applied to the problem of representing actions and generating plans.

Many examples in this book are framed as exercises, and their solutions are presented in the appendix. This organization gives the reader an opportunity to look for a solution on his own and then compare his ideas with the solution proposed in the book.

This book, as well as everything else I have written, owes much to my wife, Elena, who heroically accompanied me in long travels around the world in search for an ideal academic environment. Eventually, I found it in the Computer Science Department of the University of Texas at Austin.

In my younger years, I was fortunate to meet a few outstanding scientists and to have an opportunity to take their classes and talk to them. I learned logic from Nikolai Shanin (1919–2011), Sergei Maslov (1939–1982), and Grigori Mints (1939–2014) and artificial intelligence from John McCarthy (1927–2011) and Raymond Reiter (1939–2002). The most important influence on my professional work, next to that of my teachers, came from Michael Gelfond, an old friend and one of the founding fathers of answer set programming. He has read a draft of this book and suggested many ways to improve it. Useful comments have been provided also by Amelia Harrison, Roland Kaminski, Joohyung Lee, and Alfred Zhong and by students who took my classes on answer set programming.

Finally, thanks to Susan Evans, senior editor, with the Springer Nature's Computer Science team, who gave me the idea of converting lecture notes into a textbook.

Austin, TX, USA   Vladimir Lifschitz
May 2019

Contents

Chapter 1
Introduction

1.1 Declarative Programming

When a programmer solves a computational problem, this is usually accomplished by finding or designing an algorithm and encoding it in an implemented programming language. This book is about an alternative, *declarative* approach to programming, which does not involve encoding algorithms. A program in a declarative language only describes what is counted as a solution. Given such a description, a declarative programming system finds a solution by the process of automated reasoning. A program in a declarative language is an encoding of the problem itself, not of an algorithm.

The difference between traditional "imperative" programming and declarative programming is similar to the difference between imperative and declarative sentences in natural language. An imperative sentence is a command that can be obeyed or disobeyed: "Go to school." A declarative sentence, on the other hand, is a statement that can be true or false: "I am at school." A program in an imperative language is formed from commands: "multiply n by 2." When declarative constructs, such as equalities and inequalities, are used in an imperative program, they always occur within a command: "multiply n by 2 until $n > m$." They are used also in program specifications.

A program in a declarative language, on the other hand, consists of conditions on the values of variables that characterize solutions to the problem. Assignments are out of place in a declarative program. Such a program can be thought of as an "executable specification." Declarative solutions to computational problems are sometimes surprisingly short, in comparison with imperative solutions. Compare, for instance, two programs solving the eight queens puzzle—the declarative program on page 42 and the imperative program on pages 49–50.

Declarative programming is closely related to artificial intelligence. AI research is concerned with teaching computers to perform intellectually challenging tasks, such as recognizing visual images, understanding natural language, and com-

© Springer Nature Switzerland AG 2019
V. Lifschitz, *Answer Set Programming*,
https://doi.org/10.1007/978-3-030-24658-7_1

monsense reasoning. Turning specifications into algorithms is yet another task of this kind, and that is what declarative programming systems do for us. Work on declarative programming is related, in particular, to the theory of knowledge representation—the subarea of AI dedicated to representing knowledge in a form that computers can use.

Declarative programming languages come in several flavors. One flavor is *functional*, which includes languages such as Lisp and Haskell. A Haskell program is formed from equations, for instance:

```
factorial 0 = 1
factorial n = n * factorial (n - 1)
```

These two equations express properties of the factorial function that can be used to calculate its values.

This book is about declarative programming of another kind—*logic programming*.

1.2 Logic Programming

A logic program consists of *rules*, which are similar to formulas used in mathematical logic.

As an example, consider the following problem. We are given a table showing the population sizes of several countries, such as Table 1.1. The goal is to make the list of all countries inhabited by more people than the United Kingdom. Let us call such countries "large." This list can be generated by the logic program consisting of a single rule:

$$\texttt{large(C) :- size(C,S1), size(uk,S2), S1 > S2.} \qquad (1.1)$$

This rule has two parts—the *head*

$$\texttt{large(C)}$$

and the *body*

$$\texttt{size(C,S1), size(uk,S2), S1 > S2}$$

—separated by the "colon-dash" symbol, which looks a little like the arrow $\leftarrow$ and reads "if." The end of a rule is indicated by a period. Capitalized identifiers in a rule (in this case, C, S1, and S2) are variables. Since uk is the name of a specific object and not a variable, it is not capitalized. The symbol size in the body expresses the binary relation that holds between a country and its population size. Thus rule (1.1) can be translated into English as follows:

Table 1.1 Population of European countries in 2015

Country	France	Germany	Italy	United Kingdom
Population (million)	65	83	61	64

> A country C is large
> > if the population size of C is S_1, the population size of the UK is S_2, and $S_1 > S_2$.

This is not a command; it is a declarative sentence explaining how we understand "large country." Turning this sentence into rule (1.1) can be thought of as an exercise in knowledge representation.

The head and body of a rule are similar to the consequent and antecedent of an implication. But their order in a rule is different from what is common in logic: instead of

$$\text{if } \cdots \text{ then } C \text{ is large}$$

we say

$$C \text{ is large if } \cdots .$$

Commas separating the expressions in the body of a rule are similar to the conjunction symbol $\wedge$ ("and") in logical formulas.

To generate the list of large countries using rule (1.1), we encode the input—Table 1.1—as a collection of additional rules:

$$\texttt{size(france,65).} \quad \texttt{size(germany,83).}$$
$$\texttt{size(italy,61).} \quad \texttt{size(uk,64).} \tag{1.2}$$

A system implementing the logic programming language Prolog will load a file consisting of rules (1.1) and (1.2), in any order, and display the prompt `?-` that invites the user to submit "queries"—questions that can be answered on the basis of the given information. The query `large(C)` would be understood as the request to find a value of C that has the property `large`, and the system would respond:

$$\texttt{C = france.}$$

If the user requests another value of C with this property, the answer will be

$$\texttt{C = germany.}$$

To a request for a third solution the system will reply no (no more large countries).

To write or understand Prolog programs, one has to think not only about their meaning as specifications, but also about Prolog's search strategy. In that sense, Prolog is not fully declarative; it has an "operational semantics." Answer set programming (ASP)—the form of logic programming described in this book—is closer to the ideal of declarativism. ASP became possible after the invention of the concept of a stable model and the creation of software systems that generate stable models. These systems are called *answer set solvers*, and their operation is described in many articles, dissertations, and books. But if your goal is to *use* answer set solvers, rather than design a new system of this kind, then you do not need to know how they operate. Answer set programming has no operational semantics.

1.3 Answer Set Solvers

An answer set solver can load program (1.1), (1.2) and return an answer without waiting for a query. The answer, the "stable model" of the program, consists of all facts that can be derived using the rules of the program:

$$
\begin{array}{ll}
\texttt{size(france,65) size(germany,83) size(italy,61)} \\
\texttt{size(uk,64) large(france) large(germany)}
\end{array}
\tag{1.3}
$$

The design of answer set solvers is based on computational methods somewhat similar to those employed by *satisfiability solvers*—systems that find a truth assignment satisfying a given set of propositional formulas. We will talk later about the relationship between solvers of these two kinds, and we will see that in some cases they can simulate each other. Satisfiability solvers are widely used as tools for solving combinatorial search problems, where the goal is to find a solution among a large, but finite, number of possibilities. Such problems are ubiquitous in science and technology. Many applications of answer set solvers are related to combinatorial search as well.

Input languages of answer set solvers provide many capabilities that are not available in Prolog. We will talk here about the art of programming for CLINGO, one of the best answer set solvers available today, and about the mathematics behind the design of its input language.

1.4 Bibliographical and Historical Remarks

Lisp was specified in 1958 and is now the second-oldest (after Fortran) high-level programming language still in widespread use. The first version of Haskell was defined in 1990.

The invention of logic programming was the result of collaboration between researchers in Edinburgh and Marseille [73]. Prolog was developed in 1972 at

Aix-Marseille University and used for implementing natural language processing systems. Its name is an abbreviation for *programmation en logique* (*programming in logic*). Two monographs on logic programming [86, 114] were published in the 1980s. New work in this area is presented at annual International Conferences on Logic Programming and published in the journal *Theory and Practice of Logic Programming*.

Research on stable models started in the late 1980s [13, 40, 48, 51]; we will say more about that work in Sect. 5.9. Many extensions of the original definition of a stable model have been proposed, beginning with the paper [52] where the term "answer set" was suggested as an alternative to "stable model."

The long history of efforts to design efficient satisfiability solvers, which began with the invention of the DPLL procedure in 1962 [27], has led to the creation of sophisticated systems that can solve, in some cases, satisfiability problems with over a million atoms [42, 58].

The development in the late 1960s and early 1970s of the concept of NP-completeness and the proof of the NP-completeness of the propositional satisfiability problem [26] showed that satisfiability solvers may be used to solve many difficult combinatorial search problems. A convincing demonstration of the power of this approach [70] was provided by applying it to the problem of planning in artificial intelligence [56].

The first answer set solver SMODELS [98] was implemented in 1996. The system DeReS [22], which became available around the same time, is not exactly an answer set solver, but its functionality is similar: it implements reasoning in default logic, which is closely related to stable models (see Sect. 5.9). That early work was followed by creating the answer set solvers DLV [24, 30, 75], CLINGO, and several others.

Two papers published in 1999 [89, 97] argued that stable models can serve as the basis of a new programming paradigm, and the term "answer set programming" was introduced in the volume where the first of those papers appeared. In that sense, ASP was born in 1999. But the fact that SMODELS can be used for planning was demonstrated 2 years earlier [28]. Biannual ASP competitions are organized now to assess the state of the art [46].

The relationship between ASP and artificial intelligence is emphasized in two books on ASP with the words "knowledge representation" in their titles [10, 50]. The *Handbook of Knowledge Representation* includes a chapter on answer set programming [49], and the *AI Magazine* has published a special issue on ASP [1].

Chapter 2
Input Language of CLINGO

CLINGO is the centerpiece of the collection of ASP-related tools created at the University of Potsdam in Germany, called Potassco (for *Potsdam Answer Set Solving Collection*). Useful documentation and teaching materials, including information on downloading the latest CLINGO release and on running CLINGO in your browser, are available at the website of the Potassco project, https://potassco.org.

The description of the language of CLINGO in this chapter is sufficient for understanding and writing many interesting programs, but it is informal and incomplete. A precise definition of a number of CLINGO constructs is given in Chaps. 4 and 5. In Chap. 7 we talk about several elements of the language that are not described in this chapter.

Files containing logic programs are usually given the extension lp. The command

```
% clingo myfile.lp
```

instructs CLINGO to find a stable model of the program myfile.lp.

Exercise 2.1 (a) Save program (1.1), (1.2) in a file and instruct CLINGO to find its stable model. (b) The population of Russia in 2015 was 142 million. Add this fact to your file and check how this affects the output of CLINGO. (c) Instead of comparing countries with the United Kingdom, let us define "large" as having more than 500 million inhabitants. Modify your file accordingly, and check how this change affects the output of CLINGO.

Exercise 2.2 Consider the rule

$$\text{child(X,Y) :- parent(Y,X).} \tag{2.1}$$

(a) How would you translate this rule into English? (b) If we run CLINGO on the program consisting of rule (2.1) and the rules

© Springer Nature Switzerland AG 2019
V. Lifschitz, *Answer Set Programming*,
https://doi.org/10.1007/978-3-030-24658-7_2

```
parent(ann,bob).   parent(bob,carol).   parent(bob,dan).
```
$$(2.2)$$

then what stable model do you think it will produce?

2.1 Rules

As discussed in Sect. 1.2, a typical rule, such as (1.1) or (2.1), consists of a head and a body separated by the "if" symbol : - and with a period at the end. Rules (1.2) and (2.2) do not contain "if"; such a rule is viewed as the head without a body.

The heads and bodies of rules (1.1), (1.2) are formed from *atoms*

```
large(C),  size(C,S1),  size(uk,S2),
  size(france,65),  size(germany,83),
      size(italy,61),  size(uk,64)
```

and one expression of another kind—a *comparison*, S1 > S2. Within an atom or comparison, we see elements of three types: *symbolic constants, numeric constants,* and *variables.* They can be distinguished by looking at the first character. A numeric constant is an integer in decimal notation, so that its first character is a digit or the minus sign. A symbolic constant is a string of letters, digits, and underscores that begins with a lower-case letter. A variable is a string of letters, digits, and underscores that begins with an upper-case letter.

An atom consists of a *predicate symbol*—a symbolic constant representing a property or a relation—and an optional list of arguments in parentheses. A comparison consists of two arguments separated by one of the symbols

$$= \qquad != \qquad < \qquad > \qquad <= \qquad >= \qquad\qquad (2.3)$$

Expressions that can serve as arguments in an atom or comparison are called *terms.* The terms that we see in rules (1.1), (1.2), (2.1), (2.2) are constants and variables, but in Sect. 2.3 we will encounter also complex terms that are formed from constants and variables using arithmetic operations. In Sect. 7.5 we will talk about one more way of forming terms—the use of symbolic functions.

An atom, a rule, or another syntactic expression is *ground* if it does not contain variables. We talked above about "facts" informally; now we can say that a rule is a fact if it is a ground atom.

In Sect. 1.3 we explained why CLINGO produces facts (1.3) in response to rules (1.1), (1.2) by saying that these are the facts that can be derived using these rules. The first four of these facts are simply part of the program, but what about the other two—in what sense can they be "derived"?

This can be clarified by considering *instances* of rule (1.1)—the ground rules that can be obtained from it by substituting constants for variables. The presence of the atom `large(france)` in the stable model generated by CLINGO can be justified by the instance

```
large(france)  :- size(france,65), size(uk,64), 65 > 64.
```

of rule (1.1), which is obtained from it by substituting the terms

france, 65, and 64

for the variables

C, S1, and S2

respectively. Both atoms in the body of this instance are among the given facts, and the comparison in the body is true. Consequently this instance justifies including its head `large(france)` in the stable model.

Exercise 2.3 (a) Which instance of rule (1.1) justifies including `large(germany)` in the stable model of the program? (b) Which instance of rule (2.1) justifies including `child(dan,bob)` in the stable model of program (2.1), (2.2)?

Exercise 2.4 Which of the following ground rules are instances of rule (1.1)?

```
(a) large(france):- size(france,65),size(italy,61),65>61.
(b) large(italy):- size(italy,61), size(uk,64), 61 > 64.
(c) large(italy):- size(italy,83), size(uk,64), 83 > 64.
(d) large(7):- size(7,7), size(uk,7), 7 > 7.
```

The last four among the relation symbols (2.3) are usually applied to numbers, but CLINGO allows us to apply them to symbolic constants as well. It so happens that according to the total order used by CLINGO for such comparisons, all symbolic constants are greater than all integers. For example, the symbol `abracadabra` is greater than 7. We can verify this assertion by running CLINGO on the one-rule program

```
p  :- abracadabra > 7.
```

The stable model of this program, according to CLINGO, includes the atom p. The stable model of

```
p  :- abracadabra < 7.
```

is empty.

Stable models of some programs are infinite. Consider, for instance, the one-rule program

$$p(X) \text{ :- } X > 7. \tag{2.4}$$

The instance

$$p(8) \; :- \; 8 \; > \; 7.$$

of this rule justifies including p (8) in the stable model; the instance

$$p(9) \; :- \; 9 \; > \; 7.$$

justifies including p (9) ; and so on. The algorithms used by answer set solvers for generating stable models are not applicable to programs that contain rules like this. In response to rule (2.4) CLINGO produces an error message saying that there are "unsafe variables" in it—an indication of the fact that a program containing this rule is likely to have an infinite stable model. But in Sect. 4.5 we will apply the mathematical definition of a stable model to program (2.4), and we will see what its stable model consists of: it is the set of all atoms of the form p (v) , where v is an integer or symbolic constant that is greater than 7.

This conclusion does not reflect the functionality of CLINGO, but it is in agreement with the behavior of Prolog systems. As discussed in Sect. 1.2, Prolog does not generate all elements of a stable model at one blow. Infinite stable models are not problematic for it, and Prolog does not reject rules like (2.4). Given this one-rule program, Prolog will answer yes, for instance, to the query ?- p (10) , and no to the query ?- p (5) .

When a program contains a group of facts with the same predicate symbol, these facts can be "pooled together" using semicolons. For instance, line (1.2) can be abbreviated as

```
size(france,65; germany,83; italy,61; uk,64).
```

Exercise 2.5 Use pooling to abbreviate line (2.2).

Exercise 2.6 If you run CLINGO on the one-rule program

```
p(1,2; 2,4; 4,8; 8,16).
```

then what stable model do you think it will produce?

2.2   Directives and Comments

In addition to rules, a logic program may contain *directives*, which tell CLINGO how to process the rules, and *comments*, which are intended for humans and are disregarded by CLINGO.

A #show directive instructs CLINGO to show some elements of the stable model and suppress the others, which is often useful. For example, in the output (1.3) of program (1.1), (1.2) the first four atoms simply repeat the facts included in the program. The output that we want the program to produce—the list of countries inhabited by more people than the UK—is given by the last two atoms. We can instruct CLINGO to "hide" all atoms that do not begin with the predicate symbol large by including the directive

$$\texttt{\#show large/1.}$$

In #show directives, and in other cases when we refer to a predicate symbol used in a logic program, we append its *arity*—the number of arguments—after a slash; in this case, the predicate is unary, and its arity is 1. Specifying the arity is needed because the language of CLINGO allows us to use the same character string to represent predicate symbols of different arities. This is sometimes convenient; for instance, we can write student(jack) to express that Jack is a student, and student(jack,stanford) to say that Jack is a student at Stanford. If we run CLINGO on the program

```
p.   p(a).   p(a,b).
#show p/0.   #show p/2.
```

then CLINGO will drop the atom p(a) from the output, because its predicate symbol p/1 is different from both p/0 and p/2.

   A #const directive allows us to use a symbolic constant as a placeholder for another constant, symbolic or numeric (or for a more complex expression). For example, the directive

$$\texttt{\#const c0=uk.} \tag{2.5}$$

instructs CLINGO to substitute uk for c0 in the rest of the file. In the presence of directive (2.5), the rule

```
large(C)  :- size(C,S1), size(c0,S2), S1 > S2.
```

has the same meaning as (1.1).

   In principle, using #const directives can always be avoided, because the command line option -c can be used instead. For instance, instead of including directive (2.5) in the file we can add

$$\texttt{-c c0=uk}$$

to the command line.

   Any text between the symbol % and the end of a line is a comment, disregarded by CLINGO. Many programs that you will see in this book include comments describing the input that the program expects. The input is often provided in a separate file that consists of facts and/or #const directives. An example is given by Listings 2.1 and 2.2. The phrase

Listing 2.1 Large countries

```
1  % Countries with the population larger than the population
2  % of c0.
3
4  % input: country c0; the set p/2 of pairs (c,n) such that n
5  %        is the population of country c.
6
7  large(C) :- size(C,S1), size(c0,S2), S1 > S2.
8  #show large/1.
```

Listing 2.2 Input for the program in Listing 2.1

```
1  #const c0=uk.
2  size(france,65; germany,83; italy,61; uk,64).
```

```
    the set p/2 of pairs (c,n) such that n is...
```

in the comment on Lines 4, 5 of Listing 2.1 has the same meaning as the longer phrase

```
    the binary relation p/2 that holds between c and n
    whenever n is...
```

As customary in mathematics, we identify a binary relation with the set of pairs of objects for which that relation holds. Similarly, we will identify a property with the set of objects with that property. We can say, for instance, that large/1 is a set of countries.

If the file large.lp contains the program in Listing 2.1, and the file large_input.lp contains the program in Listing 2.2, then the command

```
        % clingo large.lp large_input.lp                    (2.6)
```

will cause CLINGO to concatenate the two files and produce the answer

```
        large(france)  large(germany)
```

Instead of adding the name of an input file to the command line, we can specify it in the program file using an #include directive. For instance, we can put the line

```
        #include "large_input.lp".
```

anywhere in the file large.lp and then drop large_input.lp from command line (2.6).

2.3   Arithmetic

In the language of CLINGO, complex terms can be built from constants and variables using the symbols

$$+ \qquad * \qquad ** \qquad / \qquad \backslash \qquad |\;|$$

for addition, multiplication, exponentiation, integer division, remainder, and absolute value. In the process of generating stable models, ground terms containing arithmetic operations are replaced by their values. For instance, in response to the input

```
p(2**5).
```

CLINGO returns the atom p(32).

The interval symbol .. can be used to form terms with multiple values. For example, the values of the term 2..5 are 2, 3, 4, and 5. The stable model of the rule

```
p(2..5).
```

consists of the atoms

```
p(2) p(3) p(4) p(5)
```

—it is the same as the stable model of the rule

```
p(2; 3; 4; 5).
```

Each of these two constructs, intervals and pooling, has its advantages and limitations. Intervals are sets of *numbers*; we cannot replace pooling in Line 2 of Listing 2.2 by an interval. On the other hand, it is not practical to replace a long interval, such as 1..100, by pooling.

The stable model of the rule

```
square(1..8,1..8).
```

consists of the 64 atoms corresponding to the squares of the chessboard:

```
square(1,1)      ...      square(1,8)
 .   .   .   .   .   .   .   .   .   .   .
square(8,1)      ...      square(8,8)
```

Exercise 2.7 Consider the program consisting of two facts:

```
p(1..2,1..4).  p(1..4,1..2).
```

How many atoms do you expect to see in its stable model?

The set of values of the term 5 . . 2 is empty, and the stable model of the rule

```
p(5..2).
```

is empty, too. The use of a term with the empty set of values, such as 5 . . 2 or 5/0, in a CLINGO program is not considered an error. CLINGO would alert you to the fact that the program contains an expression like 5/0 by displaying the message

```
info: operation undefined
```

but this is not an error message.

In Sect. 4.6 we will say more about calculating the set of values of a ground term.

Intervals can occur not only in the head of a rule, but also in the body. The comparison in the body of the rule

$$p(N,N*N+N+41) \; :- \; N \; = \; 0..3. \tag{2.7}$$

expresses that N is one of the values of the term 0 . . 3. The stable model of this rule, generated by CLINGO, is

```
p(0,41)  p(1,43)  p(2,47)  p(3,53)
```

In Sect. 4.7 we will return to this example and prove that the output of CLINGO in this case conforms with the general definition of a stable model.

Exercise 2.8 Which instance of rule (2.7) justifies the presence of p(0,41) in the stable model?

Exercise 2.9 For each of the given one-rule programs, predict what stable model CLINGO is going to produce.

(a)   p(N,N*N+N+41)   :-   N+1 = 1..4.
(b)   p(N,N*N+N+41)   :-   N = -3..3,   N >= 0.

Exercise 2.10 Write a one-rule program that does not contain pooling and has the same stable model as the program from Exercise 2.6 (page 10).

Exercise 2.11 For each of the given sets of ground atoms, write a one-rule program that does not contain pooling and has that set as its stable model.

(a)

```
p(0,1)  p(1,-1)  p(2,1)  p(3,-1)  p(4,1)
```

(b)

```
p(1,1)
p(2,1)  p(2,2)
p(3,1)  p(3,2)  p(3,3)
p(4,1)  p(4,2)  p(4,3)  p(4,4)
```

2.4 Definitions

Many rules in a logic program can be thought of as definitions. We can say, for instance, that rule (1.1) defines the predicate `large/1` in terms of the predicate `p/2`, rule (2.1) defines `child/2` in terms of `parent/2`, and rule (2.7) defines `p/2`.

Exercise 2.12 (a) How would you define the predicate `grandparent/2` in terms of `parent/2`? (b) If you run CLINGO on your definition, combined with facts (2.2), what stable model do you think it will produce?

Exercise 2.13 (a) How would you define the predicate `sibling/2` in terms of `parent/2`? (b) If you run CLINGO on your definition, combined with facts (2.2), what stable model do you think it will produce?

Exercise 2.14 Assuming that the atom `enrolled(S,C)` expresses that student S is enrolled in class C, how would you define the set `enrolled/1` of all students who are enrolled in at least one class?

Exercise 2.15 Assuming that the atom `lives_in(X,C)` expresses that person X lives in city C, and that the atom `same_city(X,Y)` expresses that X and Y live in the same city, how would you define `same_city/2` in terms of `lives_in/2`?

Exercise 2.16 Assuming that the atom `age(X,N)` expresses that person X is N years old, and that the atom `older(X,Y)` expresses that X is older than Y, how would you define `older/2` in terms of `age/2`?

Sometimes the definition of a predicate consists of several rules. For instance, the pair of rules

```
parent(X,Y)  :- father(X,Y).
parent(X,Y)  :- mother(X,Y).
```

defines `parent/2` in terms of `father/2` and `mother/2`.

A predicate can be defined recursively. In a recursive definition, the defined predicate occurs not only in the heads of the rules but also in some of the bodies. The definition of `ancestor/2` in terms of `parent/2` is an example:

$$
\begin{array}{ll}
\texttt{ancestor(X,Y)} & \texttt{:- parent(X,Y).} \\
\texttt{ancestor(X,Z)} & \texttt{:- ancestor(X,Y), ancestor(Y,Z).}
\end{array}
\qquad (2.8)
$$

This definition characterizes the relation `ancestor/2` as the transitive closure of the relation `parent/2`.

Exercise 2.17 If we run CLINGO on the program consisting of rules (2.2) and (2.8), what stable model do you expect it to produce?

Sometimes a predicate cannot be defined in one step, and auxiliary predicates have to be defined first. Consider, for instance, the property of being a prime number

between 1 and some upper bound, say 5. It is easier to define the opposite property
of being a composite number between 1 and 5:

```
composite(N)  :- N = 1..5, I = 2..N-1, N\I = 0.        (2.9)
```

(Recall that a positive integer N is called composite if it is evenly divided by
a number between 2 and $N - 1$.) Then prime/1 can be defined in terms of
composite/1 by the rule

```
prime(N)  :- N = 2..5, not composite(N).              (2.10)
```

(A positive integer N is called prime if it is different from 1 and not composite.)

Rule (2.10) is an example of the use of negation in a CLINGO program. Recall
that an atom is included in a stable model of a program, informally speaking, if it
can be derived using its rules (Sect. 1.3). But in what sense can rule (2.10) be used
to derive the atom prime(3)? About the instance

```
prime(3)  :- 3 = 2..5, not composite(3)
```

of that rule we can say that the expression

```
not composite(3)
```

in its body is justified in the sense that any attempt to use rule (2.9) to derive
the atom composite(3) would fail. The negation symbol not, which is often
used in logic programs, is said to represent "negation as failure." To emphasize this
understanding of negation, we can read rule (2.10) as follows:

> N is a prime number between 1 and 5 if
> it is one of the numbers 2, ... , 5
> and *there is no evidence* that it is composite.

Negation as failure is an important idea, and we characterize it by a mathematical
definition in Sect. 5.2. In Sect. 5.5 that definition is used to calculate the stable model
of program (2.9), (2.10). In Sect. 7.6 we talk about another kind of negation used in
logic programs, "classical negation."

The definitions of composite/1 and prime/1 above, with 5 replaced by a
placeholder and with a few comments added, are reproduced in Listing 2.3. If this
program is saved in file primes.lp then we can instruct CLINGO to find all primes
between 1 and 5 by issuing the command

```
% clingo primes.lp -c n=5
```

Listing 2.3 Prime numbers

```
1  % Prime numbers from 1 to n.
2
3  % input: positive integer n.
4
5  composite(N) :- N = 1..n, I = 2..N-1, N\I = 0.
6  % achieved: composite(N) iff N is a composite number from
7  %                {1,...,n}.
8
9  prime(N) :- N = 2..n, not composite(N).
10 % achieved: prime(N) iff N is a prime number from {1,...,n}.
11
12 #show prime/1.
```

In Line 6 of the listing, "iff" is shortened "if and only if"—a standard abbreviation in mathematical literature. The comment in Lines 6 and 7 tells us which atoms containing the predicate symbol composite/1 we expect to see in the stable model of the rule in Line 5. Including the second rule (Line 9) will not add any new atoms with this predicate symbol, of course. A comment explaining what has been "achieved" by a group of rules at the beginning of a program expresses a property of stable models of that group of rules that the programmer expects to hold also in the future, when more rules are added. Such comments help us understand the design of the program, the programmer's intentions. They also help the programmer start debugging at an early stage, when only a part of the program has been written. For example, after writing Lines 1–7 of the program in Listing 2.3 we may wish to check whether the stable model produced by CLINGO for the first rule with n equal to 5 is indeed

$$composite(4)$$

Exercise 2.18 Two integers are said to be *coprime* if the only positive integer that divides both of them is 1. We would like to generate the list of all integers from the set $\{1,\ldots,n\}$ that are coprime with an integer k. For example, if we save such a program in the file coprimes.lp then the command line

$$\% \; clingo \; coprimes.lp \; -c \; n=10 \; -c \; k=12$$

is expected to generate the output

$$coprime(1) \; coprime(5) \; coprime(7)$$

What rules would you place in Lines 5 and 10 of Listing 2.4 to get this result?

Exercise 2.19 Every nonnegative integer can be represented as the sum of four complete squares, for instance:

Listing 2.4 Coprime numbers (Exercise 2.18)

```
1  % Numbers from 1 to n that are coprime with k.
2
3  % input: positive integer n; integer k.
4
5  _____
6  % achieved: noncoprime(N) iff N is a number from {1,...,n}
7  %              such that N and k have a common divisor greater
8  %              than 1.
9
10 _____
11 % achieved: coprime(N) iff N is a number from {1,...,n}
12 %              that is coprime with k.
13
14 #show coprime/1.
```

Listing 2.5 Three squares are not enough (Exercise 2.19)

```
1  % Numbers from 1 to n that cannot be represented as the sum
2  % of 3 complete squares.
3
4  % input: positive integer n.
5
6  _____
7  % achieved: three/1 is the set of numbers from {1,...,n} that
8  %              can be represented as the sum of 3 squares.
9
10 _____
11 % achieved: more_than_three/1 is the set of numbers from
12 %              {1,...,n} that can't be represented as the sum
13 %              of 3 squares.
14
15 #show more_than_three/1.
```

$$7 = 2^2 + 1^2 + 1^2 + 1^2; \ 10 = 3^2 + 1^1 + 0^2 + 0^2.$$

But if we want to represent a given number as the sum of only three complete squares, that may be impossible. The smallest numbers that require four complete squares are 7 and 15. We would like to generate the list of all integers from the set $\{1, \ldots, n\}$ that cannot be represented as the sum of three complete squares. What rules would you place in Lines 6 and 10 of Listing 2.5 to get such a program?

Listing 2.6 gives yet another example of a pair of definitions, one on top of the other. Before defining the property fac/1 of being the factorial of n, we give a recursive definition of the binary relation fac/2, "the factorial of N is F." Note

Listing 2.6 Factorials

```
1  % Factorial of n.
2
3  % input: nonnegative integer n.
4
5  fac(0,1).
6  fac(N+1,F*(N+1))  :- fac(N,F), N<n.
7  % achieved: fac/2 = {(0,0!),...,(n,n!)}.
8
9  fac(F)  :- fac(n,F).
10 % achieved: fac/1 = {n!}.
11
12 #show fac/1.
```

that there is no "achieved" comment after Line 5. Nothing of interest is achieved in the middle of a definition.

Exercise 2.20 Consider the part of the program shown in Listing 2.6 that precedes the comment in Line 7. What atoms do you expect to see in its stable model if the value of n is 4?

2.5 Choice Rules

Each of the logic programs discussed so far has a single stable model. But in answer set programming we more often deal with programs that have many stable models. Some programs have no stable models. This is as common as equations with many roots, or no roots, in algebra.

In CLINGO programs with several stable models we often see *choice rules*, which describe several alternative ways to form a stable model. The head of a choice rule includes an expression in braces, for instance:

$$\{p(a); q(b)\}. \qquad (2.11)$$

This choice rule describes all possible ways to choose which of the atoms p(a), q(b) are included in the model. There are four possible combinations, so that one-rule program (2.11) has four stable models. The number of stable models that we would like CLINGO to display can be specified on the command line; 1 is the default, and 0 means "find all." For instance, if rule (2.11) is saved in the file choice.lp then the command

```
% clingo choice.lp 0
```

will produce a list of four stable models:

```
Answer: 1

Answer: 2
q(b)
Answer: 3
p(a)
Answer: 4
 p(a) q(b)
SATISFIABLE

Models        : 4
```

In response to the command line

```
                    % clingo choice.lp 2
```

CLINGO will respond:

```
Answer: 1

Answer: 2
q(b)
SATISFIABLE

   Models       : 2+
```

The plus after 2 indicates that the process of generating stable models has not been completed, so that the program may have other stable models.

Choice rules may contain pooling and intervals. For instance, the rule

$$\{p(a;\ b;\ c)\}.$$

has the same meaning as

$$\{p(a);\ p(b);\ p(c)\}.$$

and the rule

$$\{p(1..3)\}.$$

has the same meaning as

$$\{p(1);\ p(2);\ p(3)\}.$$

Before and after an expression in braces we can put integers, which express bounds on the cardinality (number of elements) of the stable models described by the rule. The number on the left is the lower bound, and the number on the right is the upper bound. For instance, the one rule program

$$1 \; \{p(1..3)\} \; 2. \hspace{4cm} (2.12)$$

describes the subsets of $\{1, 2, 3\}$ that consist of 1 or 2 elements:

```
Answer: 1
p(2)
Answer: 2
p(3)
Answer: 3
p(2) p(3)
Answer: 4
p(1)
Answer: 5
p(1) p(3)
Answer: 6
p(1) p(2)
```

Exercise 2.21 For each of the given programs, what do you think is the number of its stable models?

(a) `1 {p(1..10)}.`
(b) `3 {elected(ann; bob; carol; dan; elaine; fred)} 3.`

Exercise 2.22 For each of the given rules, find a simpler rule that has the same meaning.

(a) `0 {p(a)}.`
(b) `1 {p(a)}.`
(c) `{p(a)} 1.`

If the lower and upper bound in a choice rule are equal to each other then the rule can be rewritten in a different format, using the equal sign. For instance, the rule from Exercise 2.21(b) can be written as

$$\{elected(ann; \; bob; \; carol; \; dan; \; elaine; \; fred)\} \; = \; 3.$$
$$(2.13)$$

A program may contain several choice rules. For example, the program consisting of rule (2.12) and the rule

$$\{p(4)\}.$$

has 12 stable models: the six models shown above for rule (2.12) and six more, obtained from them by adding the atom `p(4)`. On the other hand, appending the rule

$$\{p(1..2)\}\ 1. \tag{2.14}$$

to rule (2.12) does not sanction including any new atoms in stable models, because each of the two values of the term 1..2 is also a value of 1..3. Rather, that rule introduces the requirement that at most one of the atoms p(1),p(2) be present in the model. In other words, combining that rule with (2.12) eliminates the last of the six answers produced by CLINGO for rule (2.12) alone.

Exercise 2.23 Given the program

```
{p; q} = 1.
{q; r} = 1.
```

what stable models do you think CLINGO is going to produce?

2.6   Variables in a Choice Rule

Choice rules may contain variables. Consider, for instance, the one-rule program

$$\{p(X)\,;\ q(X)\}\ =\ 1\ :-\ X\ =\ 1..n.$$

where n is a placeholder for a nonnegative integer. Each of its stable models includes one of the atoms p(1), q(1), one of the atoms p(2), q(2), and so on. The program has 2^n stable models; each of them describes a partition of the set $\{1,\ldots,n\}$ into subsets p/1, q/1 (possibly empty). For $n = 2$ CLINGO produces four stable models:

```
Answer: 1
q(1)  p(2)
Answer: 2
q(1)  q(2)
Answer: 3
p(1)  p(2)
Answer: 4
p(1)  q(2)
```

The rule

$$\{p(X,1..2)\}\ =\ 1\ :-\ X\ =\ 1..n.$$

is similar: each of its 2^n stable models includes one of the atoms p(1,1),p(1,2), one of the atoms p(2,1),p(2,2), and so on.

Variables can be also used in a choice rule *locally*, for the purpose of specifying the list of atoms in braces in terms of predicates defined earlier. For instance, if we defined the predicate person/1 by the rule

```
     person(ann; bob; carol; dan; elaine; fred).
```

then choice rule (2.13) can be rewritten as

$$\{\texttt{elected(X) : person(X)}\} = 3. \qquad (2.15)$$

Local variables, such as X in this example, are syntactically distinguished by the fact that all their occurrences are between braces.

Variables that are not local are said to be *global*. Substituting new values for a global variable produces new instances of the rule; substituting values for a local variable does not. For example, rule (2.15) has one instance—itself, just like rule (2.13) that has no variables at all.

Exercise 2.24 (a) Rewrite the last rule of the program

```
p(a; b).
{q(X,Y) : p(X), p(Y)} = 1.
```

without the use of local variables. (b) How many stable models do you think this program has?

A choice rule may contain both local and global variables. For instance, in the rule

```
{elected(X,C) : person(X)} = 3 :- committee(C).
```

the variable X is local, and the variable C is global.

Exercise 2.25 (a) Rewrite the last rule of the program

```
p(a; b).
q(1..4).
1 {r(X,Y) : p(X)} :- q(Y).
```

without the use of local variables. (b) How many stable models do you think this program has?

2.7 Constraints

Logic programs containing choice rules often contain also *constraints*—rules that weed out the stable models for which the constraint is "violated." A constraint is a rule with the empty head, for instance

$$:- \texttt{p(1)}. \qquad (2.16)$$

By adding this constraint to a program, we eliminate its stable models that contain
p(1). We have seen, for example, that program (2.12) on page 21 has six stable
models. Adding rule (2.16) to it eliminates the last three of them—those that contain
p(1). Adding the "opposite" constraint

$$:- \ \text{not} \ p(1) . \tag{2.17}$$

to (2.12) eliminates the first three answers—those that do not contain p(1).
    It is interesting to compare two rules: constraint (2.17) and the fact

$$p(1) . \tag{2.18}$$

In some cases, adding this fact to a program has the same effect as adding
constraint (2.17). For instance, adding (2.18) to choice rule (2.12) results in
eliminating the stable models that do not contain p(1). But generally the effect
of adding fact (2.18) to a program is different. For instance, compare the programs

```
{p(2)}.
:- not p(1).
```

and

```
{p(2)}.
p(1).
```

The former has no stable models, because both stable models of the choice rule are
eliminated by the constraint. The latter has two stable models:

```
Answer: 1
p(1)
Answer: 2
p(1) p(2)
```

In this case, adding fact (2.18) to the choice rule modified its stable models by
adding an atom to each of them.
    Combining choice rule (2.12) with the constraint

$$:- \ p(1), \ p(2) .$$

will eliminate Answer 6—the stable model that includes both p(1) and p(2).
Combining (2.12) with the pair of constraints

$$:- \ p(1) .$$
$$:- \ p(2) .$$

will eliminate Answers 4–6, because they violate the first constraint, and also
Answers 1 and 3, because they violate the second.

Exercise 2.26 Consider the program consisting of choice rule (2.12) and the constraint

$$:- \ p(1), \ not \ p(2).$$

How many stable models do you think it has?

Cardinality bounds in a choice rule can be replaced by constraints. For instance, the rule

$$\{p(a); \ q(b)\} \ 1.$$

has the same meaning as the pair of rules

```
{p(a); q(b)}.
:- p(a), q(b).
```

Exercise 2.27 Find a similar transformation for the rule

$$1 \ \{p(a); \ q(b)\}.$$

Constraints may contain variables. For instance, the constraint

$$:- \ p(X), \ q(X).$$

expresses that the set $p/1$ is disjoint from $q/1$. Adding this constraint to a program eliminates the stable models in which $p/1$ and $q/1$ have a common element. The constraint

$$:- \ f(X,Y1), \ f(X,Y2), \ Y1! \ = \ Y2. \tag{2.19}$$

expresses that the binary relation $f/2$ is functional: for every X there is at most one Y such that $f(X,Y)$.

Exercise 2.28 Given the program

```
{p(1..10)}.
:- p(2*X).
```

how many stable models do you think CLINGO will find?

A comparison in the body of a constraint can be replaced by the opposite comparison in the head. For instance, constraint (2.19) can be rewritten as

$$Y1 \ = \ Y2 \ :- \ f(X,Y1), \ f(X,Y2).$$

If the head of a rule is a comparison then that rule is not part of a definition; it is a constraint in disguise. We will return to this example in Sect. 6.1.

2.8 Anonymous Variables

Imagine a rectangular grid filled with numbers. If the atom `filled(R,C,X)` expresses that the number in row R and column C is X then the constraints

```
R1 = R2 :- filled(R1,C1,X), filled(R2,C2,X).
C1 = C2 :- filled(R1,C1,X), filled(R2,C2,X).
```

express that the numbers in the grid are pairwise distinct. In the first of these rules, each of the variables C1, C2 occurs only once. Consequently the choice of variables in these positions is irrelevant, as long as they are different from the other variables occurring in the rule and from each other. The language of CLINGO allows us to make such variables "anonymous" and replace each of them by an underscore:

$$R1 = R2 :- \text{filled}(R1,\_,X), \text{filled}(R2,\_,X). \qquad (2.20)$$

In the second rule, underscores can be used instead of R1 and R2.

To give another example, an underscore can be used in place of the variable C in the answer to Exercise 2.14 (page 15).

Underscores can be eliminated from a rule with anonymous variables by replacing them with distinct new variables. For instance, rule (2.20) can be rewritten as

```
R1 = R2 :- filled(R1,Var1,X), filled(R2,Var2,X).
```

But the process implemented in CLINGO is different: it "projects out" anonymous variables using auxiliary predicates. We can project out the anonymous variables in rule (2.20) by rewriting it as

```
R1 = R2 :- aux(R1,X), aux(R2,X).
aux(R,X) :- filled(R,Var,X).
```

Auxiliary predicates, such as `aux/2` in this example, are not shown in the output of CLINGO, so that they remain invisible to the user.

It is important to keep this detail in mind when an anonymous variable is used in the scope of negation. Consider, for instance, the program

$$\{p(1..2)\}. \\ :- \text{not } p(\_). \qquad (2.21)$$

The corresponding program with the auxiliary variable projected out is

```
{p(1..2)}.
aux :- p(Var).
:- not aux.
```

This program has three stable models:

```
Answer: 1
p(2) aux
Answer: 2
p(1) aux
Answer: 3
p(1) p(2) aux
```

These are the answers produced by CLINGO in response to program (2.21), except that the atom `aux` is not shown. If, on the other hand, we replace the underscore in (2.21) with `Var` then the response of CLINGO will be different: it will tell us that the program is unsafe.

Example (2.21) illustrates a general fact: adding the constraint

$$:- \text{ not } p(\_).$$

to any program weeds out its stable models in which `p/1` is empty.

Exercise 2.29 Given the program

```
p(1,1).
q(X) :- X = 1..2, not p(X,_).
```

what stable models do you think CLINGO is going to produce?

2.9 Bibliographical and Historical Remarks

The oldest answer set solver SMODELS [98] produced error messages similar to the "unsafe" messages of CLINGO in many cases that CLINGO justifiably considers safe: these programs have finite stable models. But even CLINGO is sometimes unnecessarily careful and rejects rules as unsafe even though they cannot possibly cause a stable model to be infinite. For example, the current version of CLINGO rejects the rule

$$p(X) :- X > 7, X < 13.$$

as unsafe; to avoid getting an error message, we have to rewrite it as

$$p(X) :- X = 8..12.$$

The rule

```
noncoprime(N) :- N = 1..n, I = 2..N, N\I = 0, k\I = 0.
```

from the answer to Exercise 2.18 has the same meaning as the shorter rule

```
noncoprime(N)  :- N = 1..n, I > 1, N\I = 0, k\I = 0.
```

because the conditions $\texttt{N = 1..n, I > 1, N\backslash I = 0}$ entail $\texttt{I = 2..N}$; however, the shorter rule is rejected by CLINGO as unsafe. There are reasons to believe that an algorithm that would correctly identify all "truly safe" rules is impossible [81].

The polynomial $x^2 + x + 41$, used as an example in Sect. 2.3, is interesting for two reasons. First, it is a "prime number generator": if you start calculating its values for $x = 0, 1, 2, \ldots$, you will get a long sequence of primes. The first composite number in this sequence corresponds to $x = 40$: $40^2 + 40 + 41 = 41^2$. Second, this is the polynomial that Charles Babbage chose, many years ago, to illustrate the idea of using his Difference Engine for evaluating polynomials [57].

There are no choice rules and no constraints in Prolog, and the first version of SMODELS did not have them either. Whenever a logic program with several stable models was needed, SMODELS programmers achieved that result using a "nonstratified" combination of rules with negation as failure, as in the program

```
p :- not q.
q :- not p.
```

It has two stable models: one of them includes p but not q; the other includes q but not p. (Incidentally, such combinations of rules are never found in Prolog programs. They would cause Prolog to go into infinite loop.) We will return to this example in Chap. 5.

The answer set solver DLV [75] uses yet another mechanism for describing multiple stable models—*disjunctive* rules, which have more than one atom in the head. Disjunctive rules are available in the language of CLINGO as well, and we will see examples in Sect. 4.4. A book [88] about logic programs with disjunctive rules (but without negation as failure) was published in 1992.

In the absence of constraints in the early days of ASP, the programmer who wanted to eliminate some of the stable models of a program would achieve that by adding a carefully constructed group of rules with nonstratified negation. With choice rules and constraints incorporated in the second version of SMODELS [99], ASP programs became more concise and easier to understand.

The tradition of using underscores for anonymous variables, as much else in the syntax of ASP programs, came from Prolog.

Chapter 3
Combinatorial Search

In a combinatorial search problem, the goal is to find a solution among a finite number of candidates. The ASP approach is to encode such a problem as a logic program whose stable models correspond to solutions, and then use an answer set solver to find a stable model.

In this chapter we discuss a few examples illustrating this approach to search.

3.1 Seating Arrangements

There are n chairs around the table. We want to choose a chair for each of n guests, numbered from 1 to n, so that two conditions are satisfied. First, some guests like each other and want to sit together; accordingly, we are given a set A of two-element subsets of $\{1, \ldots, n\}$, and, for every $\{i, j\}$ in A, guests i and j should sit next to each other. Second, some guests dislike each other and do not want to sit together; accordingly, we are given a set B of two-element subsets of $\{1, \ldots, n\}$, and, for every $\{i, j\}$ in B, guests i and j should be separated by at least one chair.

Listing 3.1 shows a CLINGO program that finds an assignment of chairs to guests satisfying these conditions, if it exists; a sample input for that program is shown in Listing 3.2. The program begins with a choice rule describing all possible ways to assign a chair to every guest (Line 12). Three constraints weed out the stable models of this choice rule that do not solve the problem, either because they assign the same chair to two different guests (Line 15), or because they separate guests who like each other (Line 22), or because they do not separate guests who dislike each other (Line 26). The rules in Lines 18 and 19 define the auxiliary predicate adj/2, which is used in the constraints in Lines 22 and 26.

We can think of the choice rule in this program as a description of "candidate solutions" to the seating arrangements problem; the constraints weed out all "bad" candidates. The definition introduces a predicate that is used in some of the constraints. This division of labor between choice rules, constraints, and definitions

© Springer Nature Switzerland AG 2019
V. Lifschitz, *Answer Set Programming*,
https://doi.org/10.1007/978-3-030-24658-7_3

Listing 3.1 Seating arrangements

```
1  % There are n chairs around the table.  Choose a chair for
2  % each of n guests so that guests who like each other sit
3  % next to each other, and guests who don't like each other
4  % sit at least one chair away.
5
6  % input: positive integer n; set like/2 of pairs of guests
7  %          who like each other; set dislike/2 of pairs of
8  %          guests who dislike each other.
9
10 % at(G,C) means that guest G is assigned chair C.
11
12 {at(G,1..n)} = 1 :- G = 1..n.
13 % achieved: each guest is assigned a chair.
14
15 G1 = G2 :- at(G1,C), at(G2,C).
16 % achieved: different guests are assigned different chairs.
17
18 adj(X,Y) :- X = 1..n, Y = 1..n, |X-Y| = 1.
19 adj(1,n; n,1).
20 % achieved: adj(X,Y) iff chair X is adjacent to chair Y.
21
22 :- like(G1,G2), at(G1,C1), at(G2,C2), not adj(C1,C2).
23 % achieved: guests who like each other sit next to each
24 %           other.
25
26 :- dislike(G1,G2), at(G1,C1), at(G2,C2), adj(C1,C2).
27 % achieved: guests who don't like each other don't sit next
28 %           to each other.
29
30 #show at/2.
```

Listing 3.2 Sample input for the program in Listing 3.1

```
1  #const n=6.
2
3  like(1,2; 3,4).
4  dislike(2,3; 1,3).
```

Listing 3.3 Seating arrangements with many tables (Exercise 3.2)

```
1   % There are n tables in the room, with m chairs around each
2   % table. Choose a table for each of m*n guests so that
3   % guests who like each other sit at the same table, and
4   % guests who don't like each other sit at different tables.
5
6   % input: positive integers m, n; set like/2 of pairs of
7   %          guests who like each other; set dislike/2 of pairs
8   %          of guests who dislike each other.
9
10  % at(G,T) means that guest G is assigned table T.
11
12  {at(1..m*n,T)} = m :- T = 1..n.
13  % achieved: for each table, a group of m guests is selected.
14
15  _____
16  % achieved: the groups are pairwise disjoint.
17
18  _____
19  % achieved: guests who like each other sit at the same table.
20
21  _____
22  % achieved: guests who don't like each other sit at different
23  %                tables.
24
25  #show at/2.
```

is typical for applications of ASP to combinatorial search. Whenever a constraint is added to an emerging program, the number of stable models decreases. When a definition is added, the number of stable models does not change, but each stable model is enriched by atoms that involve the newly defined predicate.

Exercise 3.1 What is the number of stable models (a) of the first 13 lines of the seating arrangements program? (b) of the first 16 lines? (c) of the first 20 lines?

Questions about the number of stable models, as in the previous exercise, are useful because they may help us detect bugs in the program that is being written. For instance, after writing the first 13 or 16 lines of the seating arrangements program, the programmer can run CLINGO on that part of the program for a small value of n and check that the number of stable models found by the solver matches the corresponding formula.

Exercise 3.2 There are n tables in the room, with m chairs around each table. The guests are numbered from 1 to mn, and we would like to choose a table for each of them so that guests who like each other sit at the same table, and guests who dislike each other sit at different tables. What rules would you place in Lines 15, 18, 21 of Listing 3.3 to get a CLINGO program that does it?

3.2 Who Owns the Jackal?

Each of four men owns a different species of exotic pet. Here is what we know about them:

1. Mr. Engels (whose pet is named Sparky), Abner and Mr. Foster all belong to a club for owners of unusual pets.
2. The iguana is not owned by either Chuck or Duane.
3. Neither the jackal nor the king cobra is owned by Mr. Foster.
4. The llama does not belong to Duane (whose pet is named Waggles).
5. Abner, who does not own the king cobra, is not Mr. Gunter.
6. Bruce and Mr. Foster are neighbors.
7. Mr. Halevy is afraid of iguanas.

We would like to find the full name of the person who owns the jackal.

Clues 2–5 are clearly relevant to the task of determining the full names of the men and the species of their pets. The other clues provide useful information indirectly. From Clue 1, for instance, we can conclude that Abner's last name is neither Engels nor Foster. From Clue 6 we can see that Bruce's last name is not Foster either, and Clue 7 shows that Mr. Halevy's pet is not iguana. Furthermore, the information on the names of pets in Clues 1 and 4 shows that Duane's last name is not Engels.

Listings 3.4 and 3.5 show a CLINGO encoding of this puzzle. It defines the set of candidate solutions by two choice rules, not just one as in the seating arrangements program. Another difference between these examples is that the defined predicates `first_name/1`, `last_name/1`, `pet/1`, and `answer/2` are not used here for formulating constraints. The first two are used in choice rules, and the last in a `#show` directive.

The program has a unique stable model, as could be expected.

Exercise 3.3 If we run CLINGO on the first 12 lines of this program, how many stable models do you think it will produce? What if we run it on the first 16 lines?

3.3 Schur Numbers

A set X of numbers is called *sum-free* if the sum of two elements of X never belongs to X. For instance, the set $\{5, \ldots, 9\}$ is sum-free; the set $\{4, \ldots, 9\}$ is not ($4+4 = 8$, $4 + 5 = 9$).

Can we partition the set $\{1, \ldots, n\}$ into two sum-free subsets? This is possible if $n = 4$: both $\{1, 4\}$ and $\{2, 3\}$ are sum-free. But if $n = 5$ then such a partition does not exist.

Exercise 3.4 Prove this claim.

What about partitioning $\{1, \ldots, n\}$ into three sum-free subsets? This can be done for values of n that are much larger than 4. For instance, if $n = 9$ then we can take the subsets $\{1, 4\}$, $\{2, 3\}$, and $\{5, \ldots, 9\}$.

Listing 3.4 Exotic pets puzzle, Part 1

```
1  % Exotic pets puzzle, Part 1
2
3  first_name(abner; bruce; chuck; duane).
4  last_name(engels; foster; gunter; halevy).
5  pet(iguana; jackal; king_cobra; llama).
6  % achieved: first_name/1, last_name/1, pet/1 are the sets
7  %            of first names, last names, and pet species.
8
9  {full_name(F,L) : last_name(L)} = 1 :- first_name(F).
10 {owns(F,P) : pet(P)} = 1 :- first_name(F).
11 % achieved: a unique last name and unique pet species are
12 %            chosen for each first name.
13
14 F1 = F2 :- full_name(F1,L), full_name(F2,L).
15 F1 = F2 :- owns(F1,P), owns(F2,P).
16 % achieved: the chosen names and pets are pairwise distinct.
17
18 :- full_name(abner,engels).
19 :- full_name(abner,foster).
20 % achieved: Abner's last name is neither Engels nor Foster.
21
22 :- owns(chuck,iguana).
23 :- owns(duane,iguana).
24 % achieved: iguana belongs neither to Chuck nor to Duane.
25
26 :- full_name(X,foster), owns(X,jackal).
27 :- full_name(X,foster), owns(X,king_cobra).
28 % achieved: Mr. Foster owns neither jackal nor king cobra.
29
30 :- owns(duane,llama).
31 % achieved: Duane's pet is not llama.
32
33 :- full_name(duane,engels).
34 % achieved: Duane's last name is not Engels.
35
36 :- owns(abner,king_cobra).
37 % achieved: Abner's pet is not king cobra.
38
39 :- full_name(abner,gunter).
40 % achieved: Abner's last name is not Gunter.
```

Listing 3.5 Exotic pets puzzle, Part 2

```
1  % Exotic pets puzzle, Part 2
2
3  :- full_name(bruce,foster).
4  % achieved: Bruce's last name is not Foster.
5
6  :- full_name(X,halevy), owns(X,iguana).
7  % achieved: Mr. Halevy's pet is not iguana.
8
9  answer(X,Y)  :- full_name(X,Y), owns(X,jackal).
10
11 #show answer/2.
```

Listing 3.6 Estimating Schur numbers

```
1  % Partition {1,..,n} into r sum-free subsets.
2
3  % input: positive integers n, r.
4
5  % in(I,K) means that I belongs to the K-th subset.
6
7  {in(I,1..r)} = 1 :- I = 1..n.
8  % achieved: set {1,...,n} is partitioned into r subsets.
9
10 :- in(I,K), in(J,K), in(I+J,K).
11 % achieved: the subsets are sum-free.
```

Exercise 3.5 Partition $\{1, \ldots, 10\}$ into three sum-free subsets.

The CLINGO program shown in Listing 3.6 solves the general problem of partitioning $\{1, \ldots, n\}$ into r sum-free subsets (possibly empty) whenever this is possible. The largest value of n for which such a partition exists is traditionally denoted by $S(r)$. For instance, $S(2) = 4$, and by solving Exercise 3.5 you proved that $S(3) \geq 10$. The numbers $S(r)$ are called *Schur numbers*. We can say that by running this program we estimate Schur numbers.

Exercise 3.6 How many models do you think this program has for $r = 2$ and $n = 4$?

Exercise 3.7 What is the number of stable models of the rule in Line 7?

Exercise 3.8 About a set X of numbers we say that it is *almost* sum-free if the sum of two *different* elements of X never belongs to X. For instance, the set $\{1, 2, 4\}$ is almost sum-free. If we want to describe partitions of $\{1, \ldots, n\}$ into r *almost* sum-free sets, how will you change the program in Listing 3.6?

If we run the program in Listing 3.6 for $r = 3$ and various values of n then we will see that the largest n for which stable models exist is 13. In other words,

Listing 3.7 Subsets without arithmetic progressions of length 3 (Exercise 3.10)

```
1  % Partition {1,...,n} into r subsets that do not contain
2  % arithmetic progressions of length 3.
3
4  % input: positive integers n, r.
5
6  % in(I,J) means that I belongs to the J-th subset.
7
8  {in(I,1..r)} = 1 :- I = 1..n.
9  % achieved: set {1,...,n} is partitioned into r subsets.
10
11  _____
12  % achieved: these subsets do not contain arithmetic
13  %           progressions of length 3.
```

$S(3) = 13$. In a similar way, CLINGO can tell us that $S(4) = 44$. In the next section we say more about using CLINGO for calculating Schur numbers.

Exercise 3.9 Use CLINGO to verify that $S(5) \geq 130$.

Exercise 3.10 About a set of numbers we say that it *contains an arithmetic progression of length 3* if it has three different elements a, b, c such that $b - a = c - b$. We would like to write a CLINGO program that partitions $\{1, \ldots, n\}$ into r subsets that do not contain arithmetic progressions of length 3, if this is possible. What rule would you place in Line 11 of Listing 3.7 to get this result?

3.4 Digression on Grounding and Solving

If we save the program from Listing 3.6 in the file schur.lp and execute the command

$$\text{clingo schur.lp -c r=4 -c n=44}$$

then the output of CLINGO may look like this:

```
Answer: 1
in(1,1) in(2,3) ...
   . . .
Time: 0.189s (Solving: 0.16s 1st Model: 0.16s
Unsat: 0.00s)
```

The difference between the total time, 0.189 s, and the solving time, 0.16 s, is explained by the fact that the operation of CLINGO begins with *grounding*— generating and simplifying the instances of rules that are essential for finding the stable models. In this case, the grounding time was around 0.03 s; grounding was followed by the solving phase, which took 1.16 s.

There are cases when the solving time of a CLINGO program is so large that the program is unusable. This happens, for instance, with the program in Listing 3.6 for large values of r and n. This is not surprising, because answer set solvers (and satisfiability solvers) are often used to solve intrinsically difficult, NP-hard problems. The worst case run-times of all (known) algorithms solving NP-hard problems grow exponentially with the size of the problem. But if large solving time is an issue then it may be useful to remember that CLINGO has several solving strategies, and we can instruct it to try several strategies in parallel. For example, the command

```
clingo -c r=4 -c n=45 schur.lp -t4
```

will instruct CLINGO to try solving the problem with 4 "threads," and the output may look like this:

```
UNSATISFIABLE

.  .  .

Threads          : 4                (Winner: 2)
```

Information on the "winner" tells us which thread reached the goal first.

There are also cases when the *grounding* time of a program is unacceptably large. In the case of the program from Exercise 2.19 (page 17), the solving time is negligible, but the grounding time grows quickly as n becomes larger. To understand why, look at the rule

```
three(N)  :- N = 1..n,  I = 0..n,  J = 0..n,  K = 0..n,

           N = I**2+J**2+K**2.
```

suggested in the appendix for Line 6 of the program (page 150). The instances of this rule that are identified by CLINGO as essential for generating the stable model are obtained by substituting arbitrary values between 0 and n for each of the variables I, J, K. The number $(n + 1)^3$ of such instances grows quickly with n. Significant grounding times are typical for ASP programs containing a rule with many variables, and we try to avoid including such rules in an encoding when possible.

The grounding time of the program from Exercise 2.19 can be improved using the fact that the summands in the expression $i^2 + j^2 + k^2$ can be always reordered so that $i \leq j \leq k$. Rewriting the definition of three/1 in the form

```
three(N)  :- N = 1..n,  I = 0..n,  J = I..n,  K = J..n,
           N = I**2+J**2+K**2.
```

decreases the number of instances identified by CLINGO as essential by approximately a factor of 6, and the grounding time goes down accordingly. Using the symmetry of a problem to improve the performance of an algorithm is known as "symmetry breaking." In Sect. 7.3 we will see how symmetry breaking can be used to speed up search in the Schur numbers example.

The program from Exercise 2.19 can be further optimized by exploiting the fact that the values of I, J, and K cannot be greater than $\sqrt{n}$:

```
sqrt(S) :- S = 1..n,  S**2 <= n,  (S+1)**2 > n.
three(N) :- sqrt(S),  N = 1..n,
            I = 0..S,  J = I..S,  K = J..S,
            N = I**2+J**2+K**2.
```

For some CLINGO programs, the process of grounding does not terminate at all. Given the program

$$
\begin{aligned}
&\texttt{p(0).}\\
&\texttt{p(N+2) :- p(N).}
\end{aligned}
\tag{3.1}
$$

(the current version of) CLINGO dies and has to be restarted. We will return to this example in Sect. 4.7.

3.5 Set Packing

In the set packing problem, we are given a list of n sets, and the goal is to find m members of the list that are pairwise disjoint (that is, have no common elements). A CLINGO program that solves this problem, if a solution exists, is shown in Listing 3.8, and a sample input for it in Listing 3.9.

In Sect. 7.4 we will see how CLINGO can be instructed to solve the optimization version of the set packing problem—to find the largest possible number of pairwise disjoint members of a given list of sets.

Exercise 3.11 In the exact cover problem, we are given a list of finite sets, and the goal is to find a part of the list such that its members are pairwise disjoint, and their union is the same as the union of the entire list. What rules would you place in Lines 13, 16, 19 of Listing 3.10 to get a CLINGO program that finds a solution, if it exists?

3.6 Search in Graphs

In a logic program, a directed graph can be described by two predicates, vertex/1 and edge/2. For example, the graph shown in Fig. 3.1 can be represented by the rules

Listing 3.8 Set packing

```
1  % Given a list of finite sets and a positive integer m,
2  % find m pairwise disjoint members of the list.
3
4  % input: for a list S_1,...,S_n of sets, its length n and
5  %          the set s/2 of pairs X,I such that X is in S_I;
6  %          a positive integer m.
7
8  % in(I) means that set S_I is included in the solution.
9
10 {in(1..n)} = m.
11 % achieved: in/1 is a set of m members of the list.
12
13 I = J :- in(I), in(J), s(X,I), s(X,J).
14 % achieved: the chosen sets are pairwise disjoint.
15
16 #show in/1.
```

Listing 3.9 Sample input for the program in Listing 3.8

```
1  % S_1 = {a,b,c}, S_2 = {b,c,d}, S_3 = {a,c}, S_4 = {b,d}.
2
3  #const n=4.
4  s(a,1; b,1; c,1;
5    b,2; c,2; d,2;
6    a,3; c,3;
7    b,4; d,4).
8  #const m=2.
```

```
vertex(a; b; c; d; e; f).
edge(a,b; b,c; c,a; d,f; f,e; e,d; a,d; f,c; b,e).
```
$$(3.2)$$

These rules can be viewed also as a representation of the corresponding undirected graph.

A *clique* in a graph is a subset of its vertices such that every two distinct vertices in it are adjacent. For example, the graph in Fig. 3.1 has cliques $\{a, b, c\}$ and $\{d, e, f\}$, and many smaller cliques, but no cliques of size 4. The program shown in Listing 3.11 describes cliques of a given size.

Exercise 3.12 A *vertex cover* of a graph is a set of vertices such that every edge of the graph has at least one endpoint in that set. We would like to find a vertex cover of size n, if it exists. What rules would you place in Lines 6, 9, 10, 14 of Listing 3.12 to get a CLINGO program that produces this result?

Listing 3.10 Exact cover (Exercise 3.11)

```
1   % Given a list of finite sets, find a part of the list
2   % such that its members are pairwise disjoint and their
3   % union is the same as the union of the entire list.
4
5   % input: for a list S_1,...,S_n of sets, its length n and
6   %           the set s/2 of pairs X, I such that X is in S_I.
7
8   % in(I) means that set S_I is included in the solution.
9
10  {in(1..n)}.
11  % achieved: several members of the list are chosen.
12
13  _____
14  % achieved: the chosen sets are pairwise disjoint.
15
16  _____
17  % achieved: covered/1 is the union of the chosen sets.
18
19  _____
20  % achieved: the union of the chosen sets is the same as
21  %           the union of the entire list.
22
23  #show in/1.
```

Fig. 3.1 Graph with 6
vertices and 9 edges

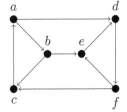

Exercise 3.13 We would like to write a CLINGO program that finds a way to color
the vertices of a given graph so that no two adjacent vertices share the same color.
What rules would you place in Lines 8 and 12 of Listing 3.13?

By running the program from the last exercise a few times, with different sets
of colors, we can estimate the chromatic number of a graph—the smallest number
of colors needed to color its vertices. In Sect. 7.4 we will see how we can instruct
CLINGO to calculate the chromatic number.

A *Hamiltonian cycle* in a directed graph is a cycle that visits every vertex of the
graph exactly once. For example, (a, b, e, d, f, c, a) is a Hamiltonian cycle in the
graph from Fig. 3.1.

An encoding of Hamiltonian cycles in the language of CLINGO is shown in
Listing 3.14. In the choice rule in Line 8, the variable X is global, and the variable Y
is local (see Sect. 2.6). The stable models of this rule (with definitions of vertex/1

Listing 3.11 Cliques of a given size

```
1  % Cliques of size n.
2
3  % input: set vertex/1 of vertices of a graph G;
4  %        set edge/2 of edges of G; positive integer n.
5
6  {in(X) : vertex(X)} = n.
7  % achieved: in/1 is a set consisting of n vertices of G.
8
9  X = Y :- in(X), in(Y), not edge(X,Y), not edge(Y,X).
10 % achieved: in/1 is a clique.
11
12 #show in/1.
```

Listing 3.12 Vertex cover (Exercise 3.12)

```
1  % Vertex cover of size n.
2
3  % input: set vertex/1 of vertices of a graph G;
4  %        set edge/2 of edges of G; positive integer n.
5
6  _____
7  % achieved: in/1 is a set consisting of n vertices of G.
8
9  _____
10 _____
11 % achieved: covered/2 is the set of edges of G that have
12 %           an endpoint in in/1.
13
14 _____
15 % achieved: every edge of G is in covered/2.
16
17 #show in/1.
```

and edge/2 added) correspond to the sets of edges such that every vertex x of the graph is the tail of exactly one edge (x, y) from that set. Adding the choice rule in Line 9 ensures, in addition, that every vertex y of the graph is the head of exactly one edge from that set. Thus adding the second choice rule does what it usually accomplished by adding a constraint—it eliminates some of the unwanted candidate solutions. This is similar to what we saw happening after adding rule (2.14) to rule (2.12) on page 22.

Every Hamiltonian cycle is represented by one of the stable models of this pair of choice rules, but the converse does not hold—some of these stable models do not correspond to cycles. Consider, for instance, the edges

$$(a, b), \ (b, c), \ (c, a), \ (d, f), \ (f, e), \ (e, d)$$

Listing 3.13 Graph coloring (Exercise 3.13)

```
1  % Graph coloring.
2
3  % input: set vertex/1 of vertices of a graph G; set edge/2
4  %        of edges of G; set color/1 of colors.
5
6  % color(X,C) means that the color of vertex X is C.
7
8  _____
9  % achieved: for every vertex X there is a unique color C
10 %           such that color(X,C).
11
12 _____
13 % achieved: no two adjacent vertices share the same color.
14
15 #show color/2.
```

Listing 3.14 Hamiltonian cycles in a directed graph

```
1  % Hamiltonian cycles in a directed graph.
2
3  % input: set vertex/1 of vertices of a graph G;
4  %        set edge/2 of edges of G; a vertex v0 of G.
5
6  % in(X,Y) is the set of edges included in the cycle.
7
8  {in(X,Y) : edge(X,Y)} = 1 :- vertex(X).
9  {in(X,Y) : edge(X,Y)} = 1 :- vertex(Y).
10 % achieved: a set in/2 of edges is selected such that every
11 %           vertex of G is the head of exactly one edge from
12 %           in/2, and the tail of exactly one edge from in/2.
13
14 reachable(X) :- in(v0,X).
15 reachable(Y) :- reachable(X), in(X,Y).
16 % achieved: reachable(X) iff there exists a path of non-zero
17 %           length from v0 to X such that all its edges
18 %           belong to in/2.
19
20 :- not reachable(X), vertex(X).
21 % achieved: all vertices of G belong to reachable/1.
22
23 #show in/2.
```

Listing 3.15 Eight queens

```
1  % Eight queens puzzle.
2
3  {q(1..8,1..8)} = 8.
4  % achieved: q/2 is a set of 8 squares on the chessboard.
5
6  :- q(R,C1), q(R,C2), C1 < C2.
7  :- q(R1,C), q(R2,C), R1 < R2.
8  % achieved: q/2 contains at most one square in each column
9              and at most one in each row.
10
11 :- q(R1,C1), q(R2,C2), R1 < R2, |R1-R2| = |C1-C2|.
12 % achieved: q/2 contains at most one square in each diagonal.
```

of the graph in Fig. 3.1. Every vertex of the graph is the head of exactly one edge from this set, and also the tail of exactly one edge from this set, but these edges do not form a cycle. To eliminate the unsuccessful candidates like this, we need to require that any vertex of the graph be reachable from any other vertex by a chain of edges from in/2. In the program, this is accomplished using the set reachable/1 of all vertices that are reachable by such a chain from some fixed vertex v0. This set is described by the recursive definition in Lines 14, 15.

3.7 Search in Two Dimensions

The eight queens puzzle is the problem of placing eight chess queens on a chessboard so that no two queens threaten each other. In other words, no two queens can share the same row, column, or diagonal. Solutions to this puzzle are represented by the stable models of the program in Listing 3.15.

In the puzzle known as Hidato, or Number Snake, you are given a grid partially filled with integers, such as this:

6		
	2	8
1		

The goal is to fill the grid so that consecutive numbers connect horizontally, vertically, or diagonally:

6	7	9
5	2	8
1	4	3

Listing 3.16 Number Snake

```
 1  % Number Snake puzzle
 2
 3  % input: positive integer n; set filled/3 of triples
 4  %        r,c,x such that the given n-by-n grid has
 5  %        number x in row r, column c.
 6
 7  {filled(R,C,1..n*n)} = 1 :- R = 1..n, C = 1..n.
 8  % achieved: every square of the grid is filled with
 9  %           a number between 1 and n^2.
10
11  :- not filled(_,_,X), X = 1..n*n.
12  % achieved: every number between 1 and n^2 is included.
13
14  (R1-R2)**2+(C1-C2)**2 <= 2 :- filled(R1,C1,X),
15                                filled(R2,C2,X+1).
16  % achieved: consecutive numbers connect horizontally,
17  %           vertically, or diagonally.
18
19  #show filled/3.
```

The program shown in Listing 3.16 solves Number Snake puzzles in which the grid is a square of size n, and the numbers go from 1 to n^2. Combining input facts, such as filled(1,1,6), with the choice rule in Line 7 is similar to the combination of fact (2.18) with choice rule (2.12), discussed in Sect. 2.7: in both cases, facts function as constraints. The inequality in Line 14 expresses that the distance between the centers of the squares (R1,C1) and (R2,C2) is less than or equal to $\sqrt{2}$; this is equivalent to saying that the squares connect horizontally, vertically, or diagonally.

Exercise 3.14 In a Number Snake puzzle with a grid of size n, k numbers are given. How many stable models do you expect to see if you run CLINGO (a) on the first 9 lines of the program in Listing 3.16? (b) on the first 12 lines?

Exercise 3.15 Cover a chessboard by twenty-one 3×1 tiles and one 1×1 tile.

The program in Listing 3.17 solves the problem from Exercise 3.15. This encoding describes all possible ways to place twenty-one 3×1 tiles on the board without overlaps; it does not mention the 1×1 tile explicitly. The expressions h(1..6,1..8) and v(1..8,1..6) represent the 48 possible positions of horizontal tiles and the 48 possible positions of vertical tiles, so that the choice rule in Line 7 requires the total number of tiles, both horizontal and vertical, to be 21.

Addition in Line 10 is applied to a number and an interval—to C and 1..2. In the language of CLINGO, this is understood as forming integers by adding C and a value of 1..2. In other words, the values of this expression are C+1 and C+2. Similarly, the values of R-(0..2) in Line 16 are R-2, R-1, and R. Applying arithmetic

Listing 3.17 Tiling

```
1  % Cover the 8-by-8 chessboard by twenty-one 3-by-1 tiles and
2  % one 1-by-1 tile.
3
4  % h(R,C) means that there is a tile at (R,C), (R,C+1), (R,C+2).
5  % v(R,C) means that there is a tile at (R,C), (R+1,C), (R+2,C).
6
7  {h(1..8,1..6); v(1..6,1..8)} = 21.
8  % achieved: positions of 21 tiles are chosen.
9
10 :- h(R,C), h(R,C+(1..2)).
11 % achieved: no overlaps between horizontal tiles.
12
13 :- v(R,C), v(R+(1..2),C).
14 % achieved: no overlaps between vertical tiles.
15
16 :- h(R,C), v(R-(0..2),C+(0..2)).
17 % achieved: no overlaps between a horizontal tile and a
18 %           vertical tile.
```

Fig. 3.2 A sensor/zone configuration for the partner units problem

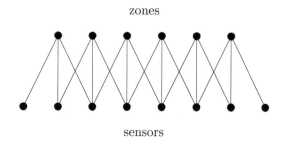

zones

sensors

operations to intervals in the language of CLINGO is discussed in Sect. 4.6 in more detail.

3.8 Partner Units Problem

In the partner units problem, we are given a set of sensors grouped into zones. A sensor may be attached to several zones. Figure 3.2, for instance, shows a set of zones with 3 sensors attached to each of them. The goal is to connect the sensors and zones to a given number of control units and to define which pairs of control units are "partners," so that two conditions are satisfied:

(i) if a sensor is attached to a zone, but the sensor and the zone are assigned to different control units, then these two control units are partners;

Fig. 3.3 A solution to the
partner units problem in
Fig. 3.2

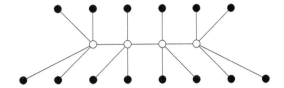

(ii) the number of sensors assigned to a unit, the number of zones assigned to a unit, and the number of partners of a unit do not exceed given upper bounds.

For example, the graph in Fig. 3.3 shows a solution for the configuration in Fig. 3.2 with 4 control units, assuming that each of the upper bounds (ii) equals 2. The horizontal edges represent the partnership relation between units.

A CLINGO program solving the partner units problem is shown in Listing 3.18, and Listing 3.19 is an input for that program corresponding to the example above.

3.9 Additional Programming Exercises

In some of the exercises above, the reader was given an outline of a CLINGO program and invited to supply the missing rules. The programming exercises in this section do not provide such outlines. In this situation, it is a good idea to start by deciding which predicates will be used to represent the input and output, and by drafting a few "achieved" comments that will help the programmer test parts of the emerging code.

Who Owns the Fish?

There are five houses of five different colors. In each house lives a person of a different nationality. Each of these five men drinks a certain beverage, smokes a certain brand of cigarettes, and keeps a certain pet. No two men have the same pet, drink the same drink or smoke the same brand. We also know the following:

1. The Brit lives in the red house.
2. The Swede keeps a dog.
3. The Dane drinks tea.
4. The green house is on the left of the white house.
5. The owner of the green house drinks coffee.
6. The person who smokes Pall Mall rears birds.
7. The owner of the yellow house smokes Dunhill.
8. The man living in the house right in the center drinks milk.
9. The Norwegian lives in the first house.
10. The man who smokes Blend lives next to the one who has cats.

Listing 3.18 Partner units problem

```
1  % Partner units problem.
2
3  % input: set zone2sensor/2 of pairs (z,s) such that z is a
4  %           zone and s is a sensor attached to it; number n
5  %           of units; upper bound unitCap on the number of
6  %           sensors and the number of zones connected to a
7  %           unit; upper bound interUnitCap on the number of
8  %           partners of a unit.
9
10 % A unit number is an integer between 1 and n.
11
12 {unit2zone(1..n,Z)} = 1 :- zone2sensor(Z,_).
13 % achieved: a unique unit number is assigned to each zone.
14
15 {unit2sensor(1..n,S)} = 1 :- zone2sensor(_,S).
16 % achieved: a unique unit number is assigned to each sensor.
17
18 partner(U1,U2) :- unit2zone(U1,Z), zone2sensor(Z,S),
19                   unit2sensor(U2,S), U1 != U2.
20 partner(U1,U2) :- partner(U2,U1).
21 % achieved: partner(U1,U2) iff U1, U2 are unit numbers such
22 %           that one of them is assigned to a zone and the
23 %           other to a sensor not attached to that zone.
24
25 :- #count{Z : unit2zone(U,Z)} > unitCap, U = 1..n.
26 % achieved: the number of zones connected to a unit doesn't
27 %           exceed unitCap.
28
29 :- #count{S : unit2sensor(U,S)} > unitCap, U = 1..n.
30 % achieved: the number of sensors connected to a unit doesn't
31 %           exceed unitCap.
32
33 :- #count{U2 : partner(U1,U2)} > interUnitCap, U1 = 1..n.
34 % achieved: the number of partners of a unit doesn't exceed
35 %           interUnitCap.
36
37 #show unit2zone/2.  #show unit2sensor/2.  #show partner/2.
```

Listing 3.19 Input for the program in Listing 3.18

```
1  zone2sensor(z(N),s(N..N+2)) :- N = 1..6.
2  #const n=4.
3  #const unitCap=2.
4  #const interUnitCap=2.
```

11. The man who has horses lives next to the Dunhill smoker.
12. The man who smokes Bluemaster drinks beer.
13. The German smokes Princess.
14. The Norwegian lives next to the blue house.
15. The man who smokes Blend has a neighbor who drinks water.

Use CLINGO to determine who owns the fish. To test your encoding, verify that it has a unique stable model.

Clique Cover

Write a program for CLINGO to cover the set of vertices of a given graph by n cliques, if possible. To test your program, use the graph from Fig. 3.1.

Bishops on a Chessboard

Use CLINGO to determine how many bishops can be placed on a chessboard so that they do not attack each other.

Filling a Grid with Letters

You are given a 5×5 grid partially filled with letters A, B, C, D, E, and with a question mark in one of the squares, for instance:

Write a program for CLINGO that determines what letter can replace the question mark if we fill the grid so that each letter is used once in each row, each column, and each of the two diagonals.

Packing Squares into a Rectangle

Write a program for CLINGO that packs a given set of squares into a given rectangular area without overlaps. For instance, if we want to pack the squares

A of size 4,   *B* of size 3,   *C* and *D* of size 2,   *E* of size 1

into an area 5 × 8 then one of the solutions is

```
A A A A B B B
A A A A B B B
A A A A B B B E
A A A A C C D D
        C C D D
```

Hitori

In a Hitori puzzle, you are given a square grid with integers appearing in all squares. The object is to darken some of the squares so that

- in undarkened squares, no number appears in any row or column more than once,
- darkened squares do not touch each other vertically or horizontally,
- all undarkened squares are connected to each other.

Write a CLINGO program that solves Hitori puzzles. To test your program, run it on the example from the Wikipedia article on Hitori (http://en.wikipedia .org/wiki/Hitori).

3.10   Bibliographical and Historical Remarks

Research on the use of automated reasoning for solving logic puzzles, such as the one in Sect. 3.2, has been conducted since the 1980s [121]. Constraint Lingo [41] is a high-level language for describing puzzles of this kind; a compiler translates Constraint Lingo representations into input languages of several answer set solvers and automated reasoning systems of other types. Work has been done also on generating ASP encodings of logic puzzles from their descriptions in English [95, 110].

Translating clues of a logic puzzle from unconstrained English into the input language of an automated reasoning system is a large step towards creating an AI system that solves puzzles. But that challenging task has also another component: the automation of commonsense reasoning steps involved in the use of the clues. The relationship between the sentences "Mr. Halevy is afraid of iguanas" and "Mr. Halevy's pet is not iguana" is that of *textual entailment* [71]: a human reading the former would be justified in inferring the latter. Writing programs capable of recognizing textual entailment is an important and difficult problem on the border of computational linguistics and artificial intelligence.

The investigation of Schur numbers started with the proof of the fact that no matter how the set of positive integers less than or equal to $\lfloor r!e \rfloor$ is partitioned into r classes, one of these classes is not sum-free [109]. (Here $\lfloor x \rfloor$ is the floor of x—the greatest integer less than or equal to x, and e is Euler's number $2.718\ldots$.) Thus $S(r) < \lfloor r!e \rfloor$. The fact that $S(4) = 44$ was established in 1965 [12]. The value of $S(5)$ is 160; it was computed in 2018 [65] using massively parallel satisfiability solving techniques. About the next two Schur numbers we know that $S(6) \geq 536$ and $S(7) \geq 1680$ [43].

The problem of detecting the cases when grounding a safe program does not terminate was studied by several researchers [18, 19, 77, 78]. The general problem is not solvable, but a partial algorithm is implemented in the answer set solver DLV. It warns the user when the termination of grounding is not guaranteed.

For any positive integers r and k there exists a positive integer n such that if the set $\{1, \ldots, n\}$ is partitioned into r subsets then at least one of these subsets contains k integers in arithmetic progression [117]. The smallest such n is called the *van der Waerden number* $W(r, k)$. The program from Exercise 3.10 allows us to estimate van der Waerden numbers of the form $W(3, r)$. For example, $W(3, 3) = 27$ [23]; this can be easily confirmed by CLINGO. It is known also that $W(3, 4) = 293$ [72].

The search problems discussed in Sects. 3.5 and 3.6 belong to the list of 21 NP-complete problems in the seminal paper on the subject [69]. To be precise, the concept of NP-completeness applies to the corresponding decision problems—determining whether a solution exists. The list includes the set packing problem, the exact cover problem, the clique problem, the vertex cover problem, graph coloring problem, and the Hamiltonian cycle problem.

The eight queens puzzle was published by the chess composer Max Bezzel in 1848. It is often used as an example in introductory programming courses. Here is the Pascal program solving this puzzle from a classical book on programming methodology [119]:

```
program eightqueen1 (output);

var i : integer; q : boolean;
    a : array[1 .. 8] of boolean;
    b : array[2 .. 16] of boolean;
    c : array[-7 .. 7] of boolean;
    x : array[1 .. 8] of integer;
```

```
procedure try(i : integer; var q : boolean);
    var j : integer;
    begin
    j := 0;
    repeat
        j := j + 1;
        q := false;
        if a[j] and b[i + j] and c[i - j] then
            begin
            x[i    ] := j;
            a[j    ] := false;
            b[i + j] := false;
            c[i - j] := false;
            if i < 8 then
                begin
                try(i + 1, q);
                if not q then
                    begin
                    a[j] := true;
                    b[i + j] := true;
                    c[i - j] := true;
                    end
                end
            else
                q := true
            end
    until q or (j = 8);
    end;

begin
for i :=  1 to  8 do a[i] := true;
for i :=  2 to 16 do b[i] := true;
for i := -7 to  7 do c[i] := true;
try(1, q);
if q then
    for i := 1 to 8 do write( x[i]:4);
writeln
end.
```

Hidato is an invention of the computer scientist Gyora Benedek. Its name comes from the Hebrew word *hida* (*puzzle*). Hidato puzzles of different degrees of difficulty are available at http://hidato.com.

Applications of the partner units problem include traffic management and security. The program in Listing 3.18 is reproduced, with minor changes, from a 2011 paper [3].

Chapter 4
Propositional Programs and Minimal Models

In this chapter and the next, we discuss the mathematical definition of a stable model. In the process, we introduce a few syntactic features of the input language of CLINGO that have not been mentioned earlier.

The first step is to review a few concepts related to propositional formulas. The presentation here is different from standard in that we write implications "backwards":

$$q \leftarrow p \quad (q \text{ if } p)$$

instead of

$$p \rightarrow q \quad (\text{if } p \text{ then } q).$$

This makes propositional formulas syntactically closer to rules in a logic program.

The reason why we need to talk about propositional formulas here is that stable models of a CLINGO program will be characterized in two steps. First, we will define stable models of a set of propositional formulas. Second, we will introduce a way to represent a CLINGO program by a set of propositional formulas, its "propositional image". For instance, the propositional image of the rule

```
r(X) :- p(X), not q(X).
```

is, according to that definition, the set of all formulas of the form

$$r(v) \leftarrow p(v) \wedge \neg q(v),$$

where v is a possible value of X, that is, an integer or a symbolic constant. Then we will say that the stable models of a program are defined as the stable models of its propositional image.

© Springer Nature Switzerland AG 2019
V. Lifschitz, *Answer Set Programming*,
https://doi.org/10.1007/978-3-030-24658-7_4

Since the set of possible values of a variable is infinite, reasoning about stable models of CLINGO programs will involve reasoning about infinite sets of propositional formulas.

As common in the literature on logic programming, truth assignments are represented here by sets of atomic formulas. For instance, assigning *true* to p and q and *false* to all other atomic formulas will be represented by the set $\{p, q\}$. This is convenient because of the role of sets of atoms in logic programming: a stable model of a logic program is a set of ground atoms.

4.1 Propositional Formulas

Assume that we are given a *vocabulary*—a set of symbols called *atomic formulas*. *Formulas* are built from atomic formulas and the logical constants $\perp$ (false) and $\top$ (true) using the connectives $\neg$ (negation), $\wedge$ (conjunction), $\vee$ (disjunction), and $\leftarrow$ (implication).

Implication binds weaker than the other connectives; for instance,

$$p \leftarrow q \wedge r \tag{4.1}$$

is understood as shorthand for the formula $p \leftarrow (q \wedge r)$.

If one of the truth values *false* or *true* is assigned to each atomic formula then the truth values of other formulas are defined as follows. The truth value of $\perp$ is *false*; the truth value of $\top$ is *true*. For propositional connectives, we use the truth tables:

F	$\neg F$
false	true
true	false

F	G	$F \wedge G$	$F \vee G$	$F \leftarrow G$
false	false	false	false	true
false	true	false	true	false
true	false	false	true	true
true	true	true	true	true

Sets of atomic formulas will be called *interpretations*. An interpretation I can be thought of as an assignment of truth values to atomic formulas: those that belong to I get the value *true*, and all others get the value *false*. If a formula F gets the value *true* for an interpretation I then we say that I *satisfies* F, or that I is a *model* of F. For instance, the empty set $\emptyset$ satisfies formula (4.1), because that formula gets the value *true* when all atomic formulas p, q, r get the value *false*.

Exercise 4.1 Assuming that the vocabulary is $\{p, q, r\}$, find all interpretations that do not satisfy formula (4.1).

Exercise 4.2 Find a formula that is satisfied by $\{p\}$ and by $\{q\}$ but is not satisfied by $\{p, q\}$.

We say that an interpretation I is a *model* of a set Γ of formulas if I satisfies all formulas in Γ.

Exercise 4.3 Assuming that the vocabulary is $\{p, q, r\}$, find all models of the set

$$\{p \leftarrow q \wedge r, \; q \leftarrow p, \; r \leftarrow p\}.$$

Exercise 4.4 Assuming that the vocabulary is $\{p, q, r, s\}$, find all models of the set

$$\{p \leftarrow q, \; q \leftarrow r, \; r \leftarrow s, \; s \leftarrow p\}.$$

Exercise 4.5 Assuming that the vocabulary is $\{p_1, p_2, \ldots, p_8\}$, find the number of models of

(a) $p_1 \wedge p_2$,
(b) $p_1 \leftarrow p_2$.

Exercise 4.6 Assuming that the vocabulary is the infinite set $\{p_0, p_1, p_2, \ldots\}$, find all models of the infinite sets

(a) $\{p_1, \neg p_2, p_3, \neg p_4, \ldots\}$,
(b) $\{p_0 \leftarrow p_1, p_1 \leftarrow p_2, p_2 \leftarrow p_3, \ldots\} \cup \{\neg p_2\}$.

The formulas in the examples and exercises above use the implication symbol $\leftarrow$ in a limited way. Some of them do not contain implication at all. Others have the form $F \leftarrow G$, where F and G do not contain implication. Formulas of these two kinds will be called *propositional rules*, and sets of propositional rules will be called *propositional programs*. We will drop "propositional" when it is clear from the context that we are not talking about rules and programs in the language of CLINGO. About a propositional rule $F \leftarrow G$ we say that F is its *head* and G is its *body*. If there are no implications in F then we say that the whole formula F is the head of the rule.

Note that a propositional program is a *set* of rules, not a list. The collection of stable models of a propositional program, as we are going to define it, will not depend on how the rules are ordered. This fact reflects a property of CLINGO: if we change the order of rules of a CLINGO program, its stable models will remain the same, although the run-time may change, as well as the order in which the stable models are generated. It contrasts with properties of sequential composition in imperative programming, where the order of components (for instance, assignments) is essential. The order of rules in a CLINGO program is only important to humans who read the program: like the availability of comments, it may affect our ability to understand the program's design.

Furthermore, a model of a propositional program is a *set* of atoms, not a list. The order in which the elements of a stable model are displayed by an answer set solver has no special significance. It may change from one version of the system to another.

4.2 Equivalence

Two formulas or sets of formulas are *equivalent* to each other if they have the same models. For instance, the set $\{p, q \leftarrow p\}$ is equivalent to the formula $p \wedge q$.

When two formulas or sets of formulas are not equivalent, this fact can be demonstrated by a counterexample—an interpretation that satisfies one of them but not the other. For instance, the formula $p \wedge q \wedge r$ is not equivalent to $p \wedge q$ because the interpretation $\{p, q\}$ satisfies the latter but not the former.

Exercise 4.7 Determine whether the given formulas or sets of formulas are equivalent. If they are not, give a counterexample.

(a) $\{p \leftarrow q, \ q \leftarrow r\}$ and $p \leftarrow r$.
(b) $p \wedge q \leftarrow r$ and $\{p \leftarrow r, \ q \leftarrow r\}$.
(c) $p \leftarrow q \vee r$ and $\{p \leftarrow q, \ p \leftarrow r\}$.
(d) $p \leftarrow p$ and $q \vee \neg q$.
(e) $p \leftarrow \neg q$ and $q \leftarrow \neg p$.

To simplify a propositional formula F means to find a propositional formula that is simpler than F and equivalent to F. (This terminology is useful, but it is not mathematically precise, because we did not define "simpler.") For instance, we can say that p is the result of simplifying $p \wedge p$. In a similar way, we can talk about simplifying a set of formulas. The art of simplifying formulas is an important part of logic, like the art of simplifying algebraic expressions in algebra, or simplifying trigonometric expressions in trigonometry. Several ways to simplify formulas containing the logical constants $\top$ and $\bot$ are shown in Table 4.1.

Exercise 4.8 Use simplification steps from Table 4.1 to simplify the given formulas.

(a) $p \vee q \leftarrow r \wedge \bot$.
(b) $p \vee q \leftarrow r \vee \top$.
(c) $p \vee \bot \leftarrow q \wedge \top$.

A set of formulas containing an atomic formula p can be simplified by replacing p with $\top$ in the other formulas that contain p, and then simplifying each of

Table 4.1 Simplifying formulas containing logical constants

Formula	$\neg\top$	$\neg\bot$	$F \wedge \top$	$F \wedge \bot$	$F \vee \top$	$F \vee \bot$
Simplification	$\bot$	$\top$	F	$\bot$	$\top$	F
Formula	$\top \leftarrow F$	$\bot \leftarrow F$	$F \leftarrow \top$	$F \leftarrow \bot$		
Simplification	$\top$	$\neg F$	F	$\top$		
Set of formulas	$\Gamma \cup \{\top\}$	$\Gamma \cup \{\bot\}$				
Simplification	Γ	$\bot$				

these formulas. Similarly, if a set of formulas contains $\neg p$ then it can be simplified by replacing p in other formulas by $\bot$.

Exercise 4.9 Simplify each of the given sets of formulas.

(a) $\{p, \ p \vee q \leftarrow r\}$.
(b) $\{\neg p, \ p \vee q \leftarrow r\}$.

A *tautology* is a formula that is satisfied by all interpretations. In other words, a tautology is a formula equivalent to $\top$. If a set of formulas contains a tautology then it can be simplified by removing it.

Exercise 4.10 Determine which of the given formulas are tautologies.

(a) $p \vee \top \leftarrow \neg q$.
(b) $p \leftarrow q \wedge r \wedge \neg q$.

A formula of the form

$$(F \leftarrow G) \wedge (G \leftarrow F)$$

can be abbreviated as $F \leftrightarrow G$ ("F if and only if G"). This formula is a tautology if and only if F is equivalent to G.

Exercise 4.11 Simplify the formula $p \leftrightarrow (p \wedge q)$.

If a set Γ of formulas contains a formula of the form $F \leftrightarrow G$ then replacing F by G or G by F in any other formula from Γ gives a set of formulas that is equivalent to Γ. Sometimes this fact can be used for simplification.

Exercise 4.12 Simplify the set $\{p \leftrightarrow q, \ p \leftarrow q \wedge r\}$.

If Γ is a finite set of formulas then we can form the conjunction and the disjunction of all elements of Γ. We will use this terminology even when Γ is empty; the conjunction of the empty set of formulas is understood as $\top$, and the disjunction as $\bot$. There is a good reason for this convention. For any list $F_1, \ldots, F_n$ of formulas of length greater than 1,

$$F_1 \wedge \cdots \wedge F_n \text{ is equivalent to } (F_1 \wedge \cdots \wedge F_{n-1}) \wedge F_n,$$
$$F_1 \vee \cdots \vee F_n \text{ is equivalent to } (F_1 \vee \cdots \vee F_{n-1}) \vee F_n.$$

If we understand the empty conjunction as $\top$ and the empty disjunction as $\bot$ then these properties will hold for $n = 1$ as well. This is similar to the convention adopted in algebra: the sum of the empty set of numbers is understood as 0, and the product of the empty set of numbers (for instance, 2^0 and $0!$) is understood as 1.

It is clear that any finite set of formulas is equivalent to the conjunction of all its elements.

4.3   Minimal Models

Definition About a model I of a formula F we say that it is *minimal* if no other model of F is a subset of I.

For instance, if the vocabulary is $\{p, q\}$ then the formula $p \lor q$ has three models:

$$\{p\}, \{q\}, \{p, q\}.$$

The first two are minimal, and the third is not.

Note that minimality is defined in terms of the subset relation, not in terms of the number of elements. A minimal model may have more elements than another minimal model of the same formula.

For sets of formulas, the definition of a minimal model is similar: a model I of Γ is called *minimal* if no other model of Γ is a subset of I.

Exercise 4.13 (a) Assuming that the vocabulary is $\{p, q, r, s\}$, find all models of the program

$$\{p \lor q, \ r \leftarrow p, \ s \leftarrow q\}.$$

(b) Which of them are minimal?

Exercise 4.14 Find all minimal models of the program

$$\{p \leftarrow q, \ q \lor r\}.$$

Note that in the last exercise the vocabulary is not specified. Since the question is about *minimal* models, there is no need to know whether the vocabulary includes any atomic formulas other than p, q, and r: such an atomic formula, if it is available, cannot belong to a minimal model.

Exercise 4.15 Describe (a) the models of the empty set of formulas, (b) the minimal models of the empty set.

Exercise 4.16 For the case when all elements of Γ are atomic formulas, describe (a) the models of Γ, (b) the minimal models of Γ.

Exercise 4.17 Find a propositional rule that has exactly four minimal models.

Exercise 4.18 It is clear that if two formulas or sets of formulas are equivalent then they have the same minimal models. But the converse is not true: two formulas may have the same minimal models even though they are not equivalent to each other. Find such a pair of formulas.

Definition A propositional rule is *definite* if

(i) its head is the conjunction of a non-empty set of atomic formulas (for instance, a single atomic formula), and
(ii) its body (if it has one) does not contain negation.

Formulas	$p \vee (q \leftarrow r)$
Rules	$p \leftarrow \neg q$
Positive rules	$p \vee q \leftarrow r \vee s$
Definite rules	$p \wedge q \leftarrow r \vee s$

Fig. 4.1 Classes of propositional formulas, with examples

A propositional program is *definite* if all its rules are definite.

The class of definite rules is a subset of the class of positive rules introduced earlier (Fig. 4.1). This class of rules is important because of the following fact:

Theorem on Definite Programs *Every definite program has a unique minimal model.*

The minimal model of a definite program can be constructed by accumulating, step by step, the atomic formulas that need to be included to satisfy all rules of the program. For instance, consider the program

$$p, \tag{4.2}$$

$$q \leftarrow p \wedge r, \tag{4.3}$$

$$r \leftarrow p \vee t, \tag{4.4}$$

$$s \leftarrow r \wedge t. \tag{4.5}$$

Which atomic formulas need to be included in any model of (4.2)–(4.5)? To satisfy (4.2), we must include p. Once p is included, the body of (4.4) becomes true, and to satisfy that rule we must include r. Now the body of (4.3) became true, and to satisfy that rule we must include q. The set of atomic formulas that we have accumulated, $\{p, q, r\}$, satisfies all formulas (4.2)–(4.5). This is the minimal model of the program.

Exercise 4.19 Describe the step-by-step process of constructing the minimal model of the program

$$p_1 \wedge p_2 \leftarrow q_1 \vee q_2,$$

$$q_1 \leftarrow r_1 \vee r_2,$$

$$r_1.$$

Exercise 4.20 Let Π be the program

$$\{p_1 \leftarrow p_2 \wedge p_3, \; p_2 \leftarrow p_3 \wedge p_4, \; \ldots, \; p_8 \leftarrow p_9 \wedge p_{10}\}.$$

For each of the following programs, describe the step-by-step process of constructing its minimal model.

(a) Π,
(b) $\Pi \cup \{p_5\}$,
(c) $\Pi \cup \{p_5, p_6\}$.

It is clear that condition (i) in the definition of a definite rule is essential: if we drop it then the assertion of Theorem on Definite Programs will become incorrect. Rule $p \vee q$ can serve as a counterexample. Indeed, it satisfies condition (ii), because it has no body, but it has two minimal models.

Exercise 4.21 Condition (ii) in the definition of a definite rule is essential also. Give a counterexample illustrating this fact.

Exercise 4.22 Consider the infinite programs

$$\Pi = \{p_1 \leftarrow p_2, \; p_2 \leftarrow p_3, \; p_3 \leftarrow p_4, \; p_4 \leftarrow p_5, \ldots\},$$
$$\Sigma = \{p_2 \leftarrow p_1, \; p_3 \leftarrow p_2, \; p_4 \leftarrow p_3, \; p_5 \leftarrow p_4, \ldots\}.$$

For each of the following programs, describe the step-by-step process of constructing its minimal model.

(a) $\Pi \cup \{p_3\}$,
(b) $\Sigma \cup \{p_3\}$.

4.4 Stable Models of Positive Propositional Programs

About a propositional rule or program we say that it is *positive* if it does not contain negation. For example, all definite programs are positive, as well as the programs from Exercises 4.13 and 4.14.

In application to a positive propositional program, the expression "stable model" has the same meaning as "minimal model." We can say that by doing Exercises 4.13(b), 4.14, 4.19, 4.20, 4.22 we found the stable models of the given propositional programs.

In view of the close relationship between stable models of propositional programs and the functionality of CLINGO, we can use CLINGO to generate the stable/minimal models of positive propositional programs. Table 4.2 relates some of the symbols found in CLINGO programs to the corresponding symbols in propositional programs. Note that the comma sometimes corresponds to conjunction and sometimes to disjunction, depending on where it occurs in the rule. The line that shows how negation is represented in a CLINGO program is not relevant now, because we are talking here about positive programs, but it will be needed in the next chapter.

To find the stable models of the propositional program from Exercise 4.13 using CLINGO, we rewrite the program as

```
p, q.
r :- p.
s :- q.
```

and instruct CLINGO to find its stable models. In the output we will see:

```
Answer: 1
s q
Answer: 2
r p
```

Note that the first rule of the program above is disjunctive—it has two atoms in the head.

According to Table 4.2, the counterpart of the propositional rule $\perp \leftarrow p \wedge q$ in the language of CLINGO is

$$\text{\#false :- p, q.}$$

In a CLINGO program, this rule has the same meaning as the constraint

$$\text{:- p, q.}$$

In other words, adding this rule to a program eliminates its stable models that contain both p and q.

Rewriting rule (4.4) in the syntax of CLINGO is less straightforward, because the body of this rule is a disjunction, and in the language of CLINGO there is no symbol for disjunction in the body. But this rule can be replaced by an equivalent pair of simpler rules; see Exercise 4.7(c).

Exercise 4.23 (a) Rewrite program (4.2)–(4.5) in the syntax of CLINGO. (b) Use CLINGO to find its stable model.

Exercise 4.24 (a) Do the same for the program from Exercise 4.19.

Table 4.2 Correspondence between symbols in CLINGO rules and in propositional formulas

CLINGO rules	Propositional rules
:-	$\leftarrow$
Comma in the body	$\wedge$
Comma in the head	$\vee$
not	$\neg$
#false	$\perp$
#true	$\top$

Exercise 4.25 Use CLINGO to find the number of stable models of the program

$$p \vee q,$$

$$r \vee s,$$

$$s_1 \vee s_2 \leftarrow s,$$

$$\bot \leftarrow p \wedge s_1.$$

Answer set solvers can be used to generate arbitrary models of a propositional program, not only minimal/stable models as in the examples above. In other words, they can function as satisfiability solvers. We will talk about it in Sect. 5.6. The other way around, a satisfiability solver can be sometimes used for generating stable models, as we will see in Sect. 6.3.

4.5 Propositional Image of a CLINGO Program

As discussed at the beginning of the chapter, our plan is to define what we mean by a stable model of a CLINGO program using the simpler concept of a stable model of a propositional program. We are ready now to do this for CLINGO programs satisfying two conditions. First, we assume that each rule of the program has the form

$$H_1, \ldots, H_m \quad :- \quad B_1, \ldots, B_n. \tag{4.6}$$

$(m, n \geq 0)$ or the simpler form

$$H_1, \ldots, H_m. \tag{4.7}$$

$(m \geq 1)$, where the members $H_1, \ldots, H_m$ of the head and the members $B_1, \ldots, B_n$ of the body are atoms and comparisons. That means, in particular, that the program does not contain the negation as failure symbol. Second, we assume that the program does not contain arithmetic operations, intervals, pooling, placeholders, and anonymous variables (see Sects. 2.1–2.3 and 2.8). Every term occurring in such a program is a symbolic constant, an integer, or a variable. For instance, rule (1.1) is a rule of type (4.6): here

   $m = 1$ and H_1 is large(C);
   $n = 3$, B_1 is size(C,S1), B_2 is size(uk,S2), and B_3 is S1 > S2.

Facts (1.2) are rules of type (4.7) with $m = 1$.

   For any program Π consisting of such rules we will describe a positive propositional program called the propositional image of Π. Then we will define the stable models of a program as the stable models of its propositional image. Since the propositional image is a positive propositional program, "stable" in this case means "minimal" (Sect. 4.4).

The vocabulary of the propositional image is the set of ground atoms of the form $p(v_1, \ldots, v_k)$, where p is a symbolic constant, and each v_i is a symbolic constant or an integer. We will denote the set of all symbolic constants by $\mathbf{S}$, and the set of all integers by $\mathbf{Z}$.

Recall that an instance of a rule is any rule that can be obtained from it by substituting constants for all its (global) variables (Sect. 2.1). Since the set $\mathbf{S} \cup \mathbf{Z}$ is infinite, the set of instances of any rule containing variables is infinite. For example, the instances of rule (1.1) are the rules

$$\texttt{large}(v_0) \ \texttt{:-}\ \texttt{size}(v_0, v_1),\ \texttt{size}(\texttt{uk}, v_2),\ v_1 > v_2. \qquad (4.8)$$

for all v_0, v_1, v_2 from $\mathbf{S} \cup \mathbf{Z}$.

Definition The *propositional image* of a program consists of the instances of its rules transformed into propositional formulas

  (i) by replacing the symbol :- and all commas in the head and the body by propositional connectives as shown in Table 4.2, and dropping the period at the end of the rule;
 (ii) by replacing each comparison $t_1 \prec t_2$ in the head and in the body by $\top$ if it is true, and by $\bot$ if it is false;
(iii) by replacing the head of the rule by $\bot$ if it is empty, and replacing the body by $\top$ if it is empty.

Note that this definition is limited to CLINGO programs satisfying the two conditions stated at the beginning of this section. A more general definition of the propositional image will be given in Sect. 4.7. Then it will be generalized again in Sects. 5.5 and 5.7, and at that point we will see that the propositional images of some CLINGO programs are not positive.

Definition A *stable model* of a CLINGO program is a stable model of its propositional image.

For instance, the propositional images of facts (1.2) are the atomic formulas

$$size(france, 65),\ \ size(germany, 83),\ \ size(italy, 61),\ \ size(uk, 64). \qquad (4.9)$$

Rule (4.8), transformed into a formula as described above, is

$$large(v_0) \leftarrow size(v_0, v_1) \wedge size(uk, v_2) \wedge \top \qquad (4.10)$$

if $v_1 > v_2$, and

$$large(v_0) \leftarrow size(v_0, v_1) \wedge size(uk, v_2) \wedge \bot \qquad (4.11)$$

otherwise. Consequently the propositional image of CLINGO program (1.1), (1.2) consists of propositional rules (4.9)–(4.11) for arbitrary v_0, v_1, v_2 from $\mathbf{S} \cup \mathbf{Z}$.

This program is definite (Sect. 4.3), so that is has a unique minimal model, and that model can be constructed by accumulating the atoms that need to be included to satisfy all its rules. Before doing this calculation, we will simplify the program. Formulas (4.11) are tautologies and can be dropped, and in formula (4.10) the conjunctive term $\top$ can be dropped. Consequently program (4.9)–(4.11) is equivalent to the propositional program consisting of rules (4.9) and the rules

$$large(v_0) \leftarrow size(v_0, v_1) \wedge size(uk, v_2) \qquad (v_0, v_1, v_2 \in \mathbf{S} \cup \mathbf{Z}; \ v_1 > v_2).$$
$$(4.12)$$

To satisfy these rules, we need to include, first of all, atomic formulas (4.9). After that, among the infinitely many rules (4.12) there will be two that are not satisfied:

$$large(france) \leftarrow size(france, 65) \wedge size(uk, 64)$$

and

$$large(germany) \leftarrow size(germany, 83) \wedge size(uk, 64).$$

Once the heads

$$large(france), \ large(germany) \qquad\qquad (4.13)$$

of these rules are added, the construction of the minimal model will be completed.

This calculation justifies the assertion in Sect. 1.3 that atoms (4.9), (4.13) form the only stable model of CLINGO program (1.1), (1.2).

Exercise 4.26 (a) Find the propositional image of the program

```
p(0,1).
p(1,2).
q(X,Y)  :-  p(X,Y),  X > 0,  Y > 0.
```

(b) Simplify it. (c) Describe the step-by-step process of constructing its minimal model. (d) Check that your answer is in agreement with the output of CLINGO.

Exercise 4.27 (a) Find the propositional image of the program consisting of rules (2.1), (2.2), (2.8) (pages 7 and 15). (b) Describe the step-by-step process of constructing its minimal model.

Exercise 4.28 (a) Find the propositional image of the program

```
p(1), p(2), p(3).
:- p(X), X > 2.
```

(b) Simplify it. (c) Find all its minimal models. (d) Check that your answer is in agreement with the output of CLINGO.

The above definition of a stable model is applicable even the program is unsafe. For instance, the propositional image of program (2.4) on page 9 consists of the rules

$$p(v) \leftarrow \top \quad \text{for all } v \in \mathbf{S} \cup \mathbf{Z} \text{ such that } v > 7,$$
$$p(v) \leftarrow \bot \quad \text{for all } v \in \mathbf{S} \cup \mathbf{Z} \text{ such that } v \leq 7.$$

Its only minimal model is obviously the set of all atoms $p(v)$ with $v > 7$, as we claimed in Sect. 2.1.

Exercise 4.29 (a) Find the propositional image of the unsafe program

```
p(a).
q(X,Y) :- p(X).
```

(b) Describe the step-by-step process of constructing its minimal model.

4.6 Values of a Ground Term

In the next section, the definition of the propositional image is extended to programs that may contain arithmetic operations and intervals. We will see there that in this more general setting the process of constructing the propositional image includes an additional step—replacing terms by their values. For instance, the propositional image of the fact

$$p(2*2).$$

is the atomic formula $p(4)$.

But first we need to talk about values of ground terms that may occur in such programs. The exact meaning of this concept is not so easy to define, for several reasons. First, a ground term may have many values; for instance, the values of `1..3` are 1, 2, 3. Second, a ground term may have no values: for instance, `1/0` has no values, and the term `abracadabra+7` has no values either. Third, as we saw in Sect. 3.7, the language of CLINGO allows us to apply arithmetic operations to intervals. In fact, when we construct a ground term from constants, applying arithmetic operations and forming intervals may follow each other any number of times in any order.

We can clarify this issue by defining the set of *values* of a ground term t that does not contain placeholders. The definition is recursive, and it consists of four clauses:

Definition

1. If t is a symbolic constant or an integer then the only value of t is t itself.
2. If t is $t_1 \circ t_2$, where $\circ$ is an arithmetic operation, then the values of t are integers of the form $n_1 \circ n_2$, where the integer n_1 is a value of t_1, and the integer n_2 is a value of t_2. (Table 4.3 shows how to translate symbols for arithmetic operations in CLINGO into standard algebraic notation.)
3. If t is $|t_1|$ then the values of t are integers of the form $|n_1|$, where the integer n_1 is a value of t_1.
4. If t is $t_1..t_2$ then the values of t are the integers n for which there exist integers n_1 and n_2 such that

   - n_1 is a value of t_1,
   - n_2 is a value of t_2,
   - $n_1 \leq n \leq n_2$.

For instance, the only value of $2*2$ is 4, because the only value of 2 is 2, and $2 \cdot 2 = 4$. The set of values of $2/0$ is empty, because division by 0 is undefined. The set of values of $2*a$ is empty as well, because the only value of the symbolic constant a is not an integer. The same goes for $2..a$.

It is clear that every value of a ground term is either a symbolic constant (if the term itself is a symbolic constant) or an integer.

Exercise 4.30 Determine for which of the following terms the set of values is empty.

(a) `6..5`.
(b) `a..(a+1)`.
(c) `2**(-2)`.

Exercise 4.31 Find all values of the term `(2..4)*(2..4)`.

Exercise 4.32 Find a ground term (a) with the values 1, 3, 9; (b) with the values 22, 32, 42.

Table 4.3 Correspondence between symbols for arithmetic operations in CLINGO terms and in standard algebraic notation

CLINGO terms	Algebraic notation
$m*n$	$m \cdot n$
m/n	$\lfloor m/n \rfloor$
$m \backslash n$	$m - n \cdot \lfloor m/n \rfloor$
$m**n$	$\lfloor m^n \rfloor$

The symbol $\lfloor x \rfloor$ denotes the floor of a real number x, that is, the largest integer less than or equal to x. The use of this symbol in the last line is needed because n can be negative; then m^n is a fraction

4.7 More on Propositional Images

We will define now the concept of a stable model for CLINGO programs consisting of rules of forms (4.6) and (4.7) that may contain arithmetic operations and intervals (but no pooling, placeholders, or anonymous variables). The *propositional image* of such a program is formed by the process described in Sect. 4.5, with clause (ii) modified as follows:

(ii′) by replacing each atom and each comparison in every rule by its propositional image as described in Table 4.4.

According to Table 4.4, the same expression may correspond to different formulas depending on whether it occurs in the head or in the body. For instance, the propositional image of the atom p(1..2) in the head of a rule is the conjunction $p(1) \wedge p(2)$, but the propositional image of the same atom in the body of a rule is the disjunction $p(1) \vee p(2)$.

To take another example, the propositional image of the atom p(1/0) in the head is the empty conjunction $\top$, but the propositional image of the same atom in the body is the empty disjunction $\bot$ (see the discussion of the empty conjunction and empty disjunction at the end of Sect. 4.2). As a result, the propositional image of any CLINGO rule with p(1/0) in the head is a tautology, and the propositional image of a rule containing p(1/0) in the body is a tautology as well. It follows that if a CLINGO rule contains the atom p(X/Y) anywhere, in the head or in the body, the formulas contributed to the propositional image of the rule by substituting 1 for X and 0 for Y are tautologies and can be disregarded in the process of constructing the minimal model.

The propositional image of the comparison 1..2 = 2..3 in the head is $\bot$ (because it is not true that the terms 1..2 and 2..3 have exactly the same values), but the propositional image of the same comparison in the body is $\top$ (because these terms have one value in common).

On the other hand, if each of the terms $t_1, \ldots, t_k$ is a symbolic constant or an integer, as in Sect. 4.5, then the only value of t_i is t_i itself, so that the conjunction in the first line of Table 4.4 is the single atom $p(t_1, \ldots, t_k)$, and the disjunction in

Table 4.4 Propositional images of ground atoms and comparisons

Expression	Propositional image
atom $p(t_1, \ldots, t_k)$ in the head	Conjunction of all formulas of the form $p(v_1, \ldots, v_k)$ where v_i is a value of t_i ($i = 1, \ldots, k$)
atom $p(t_1, \ldots, t_k)$ in the body	Disjunction of all formulas of the form $p(v_1, \ldots, v_k)$ where v_i is a value of t_i ($i = 1, \ldots, k$)
comparison $t_1 \prec t_2$ in the head	$\top$ if for every value v_1 of t_1 and every value v_2 of t_2, $v_1 \prec v_2$; $\bot$ otherwise
comparison $t_1 \prec t_2$ in the body	$\top$ if for some value v_1 of t_1 and some value v_2 of t_2, $v_1 \prec v_2$; $\bot$ otherwise

Here p is a symbolic constant, each t_i is a ground term, and $\prec$ is a comparison symbol the second line of the table is the same atom. Similarly, if each of the terms t_1, t_2 is a symbolic constant or an integer then the truth value described in the third line of the table is $\top$ or $\bot$ depending on whether the condition $t_1 \prec t_2$ is true or false, and the value in the fourth line is calculated in the same way. We conclude that the definition of the propositional image above has the same meaning as the definition in Sect. 4.5 when the program contains neither arithmetical operations nor intervals.

If each of the terms $t_1, \ldots, t_k$ is formed from integers using addition, subtraction, and multiplication, then t_i has a unique value v_i, so that the conjunction in the first line of Table 4.4 is the atom $p(v_1, \ldots, v_k)$, and so is the disjunction in the second line. For instance, the propositional image of p(2*2) is $p(4)$ no matter whether this atom occurs in the head or in the body.

Consider, for instance, one-rule program (2.7) (page 14). Its propositional image consists of the rules

$$p(0, 41) \leftarrow \top,$$
$$p(1, 43) \leftarrow \top,$$
$$p(2, 47) \leftarrow \top,$$
$$p(3, 53) \leftarrow \top,$$
$$p(n, m) \leftarrow \bot \quad \text{for all } n \in \mathbf{Z} \setminus \{0, \ldots, 3\}, \text{ where } m \text{ is the value of } n^2 + n + 41,$$
$$\top \leftarrow \bot.$$

$$(4.14)$$

(The last formula corresponds to the instances of (2.7) obtained by substituting symbolic constants for N.) The rules in the last two lines are tautologies, and the other rules can be equivalently written as

$$p(0, 41), \quad p(1, 43), \quad p(2, 47), \quad p(3, 53).$$

Consequently these atoms form the only stable model of (2.7), in accordance with the claim about this program made in Sect. 2.3.

The propositional image of the program

```
p(2).
p(a).
q(X+1) :- p(X).
```

consists of the formulas

$$p(2),$$
$$p(a),$$
$$q(m) \leftarrow p(n) \quad \text{for all } n \in \mathbf{Z}, \text{ where } m \text{ is the value of } n + 1,$$
$$\top \leftarrow q(v) \quad \text{for all } v \in \mathbf{S}.$$

The rules in the last line are tautologies and can be dropped. The stable model of the program is $\{p(2), p(a), q(3)\}$.

Exercise 4.33 For each of the given rules, find its propositional image. Which of the propositional images are tautologies?

(a) `square(1..2,1..2).`
(b) `q :- square(1..2,1..2).`
(c) `square(abra..cadabra,abra..cadabra).`
(d) `q :- square(abra..cadabra,abra..cadabra).`

Exercise 4.34 (a) Find the propositional image of the program

```
p(1).
q :- p(1..3).
```

(b) Find the minimal model of the propositional image. (c) Check that your answer is in agreement with the output of CLINGO.

Exercise 4.35 Do the same for the one-rule program

$$p(1/N) \; :- \; N = 0..1.$$

Exercise 4.36 Find the propositional image of the program

```
p(1..3).
q(X)  :- p(X), X = 2..4.
```

(b) Simplify it. (c) Describe the step-by-step process of constructing its minimal model. (d) Check that your answer is in agreement with the output of CLINGO.

Exercise 4.37 Do the same for the program

```
p(1,1..2).
q(X,Y)  :- p(X,Y), X != Y.
q(X,Y)  :- q(Y,X).
```

Exercise 4.38 Do the same for the program

```
p(1..3).
q(N-1..N+1)  :- p(N).
```

Exercise 4.39 (a) Find the propositional image of the program

```
p(1..3).
X = 1 :- p(X).
```

(b) Find all its minimal models.

Exercise 4.40 (a) Find the propositional image of the unsafe program

```
p(1).
q(X)  :- p((-1)**X).
```

(b) Describe the step-by-step process of constructing its minimal model.

We have seen that the mathematical definition of a stable model is applicable to unsafe programs, such as program (2.4) on page 9 and the program from Exercise 4.40. It is applicable also to safe programs for which grounding does not terminate, such as program (3.1) on page 37. The propositional image of that program consists of the rules

$$p(0),$$
$$p(m) \leftarrow p(n) \qquad \text{for all } n \in \mathbf{Z}, \text{ where } m \text{ is the value of } n + 2,$$
$$\top \leftarrow p(v) \qquad \text{for all } v \in \mathbf{S}.$$

The rules in the last line are tautologies and can be dropped. The result is a definite program, and the process of constructing its minimal model involves infinitely many steps: we include $p(0)$, then add $p(2)$, then add $p(4)$, and so on. This is similar to what we saw in Exercise 4.22(b) on page 58.

Programs (2.4) and (3.1) are similar to each other in the sense that each of them has a unique infinite stable model, but CLINGO responds to these programs in different ways: it rejects the former as unsafe, but it tries—unsuccessfully—to ground the latter. The difference can be explained in terms of the process of accumulating the ground atoms that need to be included in the minimal model of the propositional image. With (2.4) and similar unsafe programs, the set of accumulated atoms becomes infinite after several steps. In case of (3.1), the set of accumulated atoms remains finite at every step, and the minimal model turns out to be infinite only because the number of steps is infinite. Such programs are treated by CLINGO as safe.

4.8 Bibliographical and Historical Remarks

The use of truth tables for defining the semantics of propositional connectives was invented in the 1920s [105, 120]. The truth tables given in Sect. 4.1 are considered now standard, or "classical" (except that we use here the left arrow for implication).

The truth table for implication may look puzzling: why is the value *false* assigned to $F \leftarrow G$ when the value of F is *false* and the value of G is *true*, whereas the value *true* appears in the other three lines of the table? This choice can be justified by the fact that in mathematics, to give a counterexample to a claim of the form "F if G" we need to make sure that F is false and G is true; we need to show, in other words, that this implication is in the "false" line of the truth table. This semantics makes implication similar to disjunction—the other connective that has *false* in one line of the truth table out of four. According to the classical semantics, the two connectives can be expressed in terms of each other using negation:

$$F \leftarrow G \text{ is equivalent to } F \vee \neg G,$$
$$F \vee G \text{ is equivalent to } F \leftarrow \neg G.$$

The classical truth table for implication is the best possible choice as long as we intend to characterize the meaning of implication in terms of two truth values. But it describes only one of many meanings of the word "if" [62].

Logical minimization of the kind described in this chapter plays an important part in the theory of "nonmonotonic reasoning." This term describes the situations when reasoners draw tentative conclusions that may be retracted on the basis of further evidence. Reasoning found in mathematical proofs is monotonic: when a theorem is derived from a set of axioms, adding more axioms will not invalidate the proof. (This is so even if extending the set of axioms makes it inconsistent: in this case, every proposition becomes a theorem, including the theorems proved earlier.) But commonsense reasoning, practiced in everyday life, is often nonmonotonic. For example, we often deal with lists that are presumed to be complete. Conclusions based on such an assumption may need to be retracted when we get additional information. Something like this happened when Prolog and CLINGO told us, in response to rules (1.1), (1.2), that in 2015 there were two countries in Europe populated by more people than the United Kingdom. We realized that the number of such countries is actually three when we took into account the fact that Russia is a European country (Exercise 2.1 on page 7).

Theory of nonmonotonic reasoning became an active area of research after the publication of the special issue of the journal *Artificial Intelligence* on nonmonotonic reasoning in 1980 [2]. One of the mathematical models of nonmonotonic reasoning described in that journal used the syntactic transformation called *circumscription* [91, 92]. To give an example, the result of applying this transformation to the formula

$$p(a) \wedge p(b) \wedge q(c) \tag{4.15}$$

is a formula that can be equivalently written as the first-order sentence

$$\forall X (p(X) \leftrightarrow X = a \vee X = b) \wedge \forall X (q(X) \leftrightarrow X = c). \tag{4.16}$$

Formula (4.15) expresses that a and b are elements of the set p, and c is an element of q; the result (4.16) of "circumscribing p and q" in that formula expresses that these lists of elements are complete, so that a and b are the only elements of p, and c is the only element of q. This is similar to what happens when we apply the definition of the minimal model given in this chapter to formula (4.15): in the minimal model

$$\{p(a), p(b), q(c)\}$$

of that formula, the atoms $p(c)$, $q(a)$ and $q(b)$ are false, so that c does not belong to p, and a, b do not belong to q.

Interaction between the semantics of logic programs and the theory of nonmonotonic reasoning is the theme of biannual international conferences on logic programming and nonmonotonic reasoning that have been held in America and

Europe since 1991. We will return to this subject in connection with the semantics of negation as failure in the next chapter, and in connection with the frame problem in Chap. 8.

The discussion of ground terms in Sect. 4.6 follows the account of the semantics of CLINGO published in 2015 [44]. The explanation of the difference between two kinds of programs with infinite stable models is based on the theory of safe rules proposed a year later [81].

Chapter 5
Programs with Negation

Our next goal is to extend the definition of a stable model from Sect. 4.4 to propositional programs that contain negation, and to apply this generalization to CLINGO programs with negation and choice. We begin with an informal discussion of a few examples.

5.1 Examples

Consider the propositional program

$$
\begin{aligned}
&p, \\
&q, \\
&r \leftarrow p \wedge \neg s, \\
&s \leftarrow q.
\end{aligned}
\tag{5.1}
$$

One of its rules contains negation, so that the expression "stable model" in application to this program does not have the same meaning as "minimal model." How do we want to understand stability in this case?

The answer to this question adopted in answer set programming is based on the idea of a self-verifying conjecture. Consider the conjecture that

$$\{p, q, s\} \text{ is a stable model of program (5.1)}. \tag{5.2}$$

Since the interpretation $\{p, q, s\}$ does not satisfy the subformula $\neg s$ of the third rule, that interpretation—under the conjecture that we are exploring—is also a stable model of the program obtained from (5.1) replacing $\neg s$ with $\bot$:

© Springer Nature Switzerland AG 2019
V. Lifschitz, *Answer Set Programming*,
https://doi.org/10.1007/978-3-030-24658-7_5

$$p,$$
$$q,$$
$$r \leftarrow p \wedge \bot,$$
$$s \leftarrow q.$$
(5.3)

Program (5.3) is definite, and its minimal model is $\{p, q, s\}$, which is exactly the interpretation that we started with. We can say that conjecture (5.2) is self-verifying, in the sense that after using it to convert program (5.1) into definite program (5.3) we could confirm it by calculating the minimal model of that definite program.

Interpretation $\{p, q, s\}$ is the only set of atoms that is confirmed as a stable model of (5.1) by this process of self-verification. No other interpretation matches the minimal model of the corresponding definite program. Sometimes the minimal model will be too large, sometimes too small, but it will not be exactly the same as the interpretation that we started with. For instance, the conjecture that $\emptyset$ is a stable model of program (5.1) leads to replacing $\neg s$ by $\top$, because $\emptyset$ satisfies $\neg s$. The definite program obtained from (5.1) after this replacement is

$$p,$$
$$q,$$
$$r \leftarrow p \wedge \top,$$
$$s \leftarrow q.$$
(5.4)

The minimal model $\{p, q, r, s\}$ of this program is different from $\emptyset$; no match. To take another example, the conjecture that $\{p, q, r, s\}$ is a stable model leads to transforming (5.1) into (5.3). The minimal model $\{p, q, s\}$ of this definite program is different from $\{p, q, r, s\}$; no match again.

The conclusion that $\{p, q, s\}$ is the only stable model of program (5.1) is in agreement with the answer produced by CLINGO if we run it on the input

```
p.
q.
r :- p, not s.
s :- q.
```

Consider now the program

$$p \leftarrow \neg q,$$
$$q \leftarrow \neg p,$$
$$r \leftarrow p,$$
$$r \leftarrow q.$$
(5.5)

The conjecture

$\{p, r\}$ is a stable model of program (5.5)

is self-verifying. Indeed, the interpretation $\{p, r\}$ satisfies $\neg q$ and does not satisfy $\neg p$; accordingly, we turn (5.5) into the definite program

$$
\begin{aligned}
p &\leftarrow \top, \\
q &\leftarrow \bot, \\
r &\leftarrow p, \\
r &\leftarrow q,
\end{aligned}
\tag{5.6}
$$

and the minimal model of this program is $\{p, r\}$. A similar calculation shows that the conjecture

$\{q, r\}$ is a stable model of program (5.5)

is self-verifying as well. The program has two stable models.

5.2 Stable Models of a Propositional Program

The general definition of a stable model below uses the following terminology. A *critical part* of a propositional formula F is a subformula of F that has the form $\neg G$ and is not contained in a larger subformula that has this form. In the rules of program (5.1), for instance, we see one critical part: the subformula $\neg s$ of the third rule. The rules of program (5.5) have two critical parts: $\neg q$ in the first rule and $\neg p$ in the second. In the rule

$$
p \leftarrow \neg\neg p
\tag{5.7}
$$

the only critical part is $\neg\neg p$; the subformula $\neg p$ is not critical, because it is contained in a larger subformula that begins with negation. If F has the form $\neg G$ then the only critical part of F is F itself.

Definition The *reduct* of a propositional rule F relative to an interpretation I is the positive rule obtained from F by substituting $\top$ for each critical part that is satisfied by I, and substituting $\bot$ for every other critical part. The reduct of a propositional program Π relative to I is the positive program obtained from Π by the same process.

For instance, the reduct of program (5.1) relative to an interpretation I is (5.3) if I does not satisfy $\neg s$, and (5.4) if it does. The reduct of program (5.5) relative to the interpretation $\{p, r\}$ is (5.6).

Definition Let Π be a propositional program, and let I be an interpretation. If I is a minimal model of the reduct of Π relative to I then we say that I is a *stable model* of Π.

Exercise 5.1 (a) Prove that $\{p, q, r\}$ is a stable model of the program

$$p,$$
$$q,$$
$$r \leftarrow p \wedge \neg s,$$

obtained from program (5.1) by dropping the last rule. (b) Prove that this program has no other stable models.

Let us find now all stable models of the program

$$p \vee q,$$
$$r \leftarrow \neg p. \tag{5.8}$$

Take an arbitrary interpretation I, and consider two cases. *Case 1:* $p \in I$. The reduct of the program relative to I is

$$p \vee q,$$
$$r \leftarrow \bot.$$

It has two minimal models, $\{p\}$ and $\{q\}$. The former satisfies the condition $p \in I$ that characterizes Case 1, so that it is a stable model of (5.8). *Case 2:* $p \notin I$. The reduct of the program relative to I is

$$p \vee q,$$
$$r \leftarrow \top.$$

It has two minimal models, $\{p, r\}$ and $\{q, r\}$. The latter satisfies the condition $p \notin I$ that characterizes Case 2, so that it is a stable model of (5.8). We conclude that this program has two stable models, $\{p\}$ and $\{q, r\}$.

Exercise 5.2 (a) Find all stable models of the program

$$p \leftarrow \neg p.$$

(b) Check that the result of your calculation is in agreement with the output of CLINGO.

Exercise 5.3 Do the same for the program

$$p \vee q,$$
$$\bot \leftarrow p \wedge \neg q.$$

The program

$$p \leftarrow \neg q,$$
$$q \leftarrow \neg p$$

contains negations of two atoms, so that four cases need to be considered in the process of calculating its stable models. Take any interpretation I. *Case 1: $p, q \in I$.* The reduct is

$$p \leftarrow \bot,$$
$$q \leftarrow \bot.$$

The minimal model $\emptyset$ does not satisfy the condition characterizing this case. *Case 2: $p \in I, q \notin I$.* The reduct is

$$p \leftarrow \top,$$
$$q \leftarrow \bot.$$

The minimal model $\{p\}$ satisfies the condition characterizing this case, so that $\{p\}$ is a stable model of the given program. *Case 3: $p \notin I, q \in I$.* A similar calculation gives the stable model $\{q\}$. *Case 4: $p, q \notin I$.* The reduct is

$$p \leftarrow \top,$$
$$q \leftarrow \top.$$

The minimal model $\{p, q\}$ does not satisfy the condition characterizing this case. Consequently the program has two stable models.

Exercise 5.4   (a)   Find all stable models of the program

$$p \leftarrow \neg q,$$
$$q \leftarrow \neg p,$$
$$p \leftarrow q,$$
$$q \leftarrow p.$$

(b)   Check that the result of your calculation is in agreement with the output of CLINGO.

The process of calculating stable models used in the examples above becomes impractical when the program contains many critical parts, because the number of reducts of a program becomes large. Fortunately, the study of stable models has led to the discovery of theorems that allow us to approach the problem of calculating stable models in other ways, and some of these theorems are discussed below.

The use of the term "stable *model*" is justified by the fact that every stable model of a propositional program is indeed one of its models. In other words, every stable model satisfies all rules of the program. This property of stable models is not immediately obvious: the definition only shows that a stable model I of a program satisfies the *reduct* of the program relative to I. But any stable model of a program satisfies the program itself as well, in view of the following theorem:

Theorem on Reducts *An interpretation I satisfies a propositional program Π if and only if it satisfies the reduct of Π relative to I.*

For example, the interpretation $\{q\}$ satisfies both the one-rule program $p \leftarrow \neg q$ and its reduct $p \leftarrow \bot$ (which is a tautology); the interpretation $\emptyset$ satisfies neither $p \leftarrow \neg q$ nor its reduct $p \leftarrow \top$.

From Theorem on Reducts we can conclude that the stable models of a propositional program can be characterized as follows: an interpretation I is a stable model of Π if and only if

(i) I is a model of Π, and
(ii) no proper subset of I is a model of the reduct of Π relative to I.

In the special case when the given program is positive, its stable models in the sense of the definition above are exactly its minimal models. This is because the reduct of a positive program Π relative to any interpretation is Π itself, so that the condition "I is a minimal model of the reduct of Π relative to I" means simply that I is a minimal model of Π. This observation justifies the claim in Sect. 4.4 that in application to models of a positive propositional program, "stable" has the same meaning as "minimal."

5.3   Stable Models as Fixpoints

In this section we talk about propositional programs satisfying the following condition:

(α) the head of every rule of the program is an atomic formula.

This condition is satisfied, for instance, for programs (5.1), (5.5), and (5.7), but is not satisfied for program (5.8): the head of the first rule of that program is a disjunction.

Stable models of programs satisfying condition α are related to the concept of a fixpoint. A *fixpoint* of a function is an element of the function's domain that is mapped by the function to itself. In other words, fixpoints of a function f are roots of the equation $f(x) = x$. For example, 2 is a fixpoint of the function $f(x) = 3x-4$, because it is a root of the equation $3x - 4 = x$. The function $f(x) = x^2$ has two fixpoints, 0 and 1.

The concept of a fixpoint is not limited to functions that operate on numbers. Consider, for instance, the function f with the domain consisting of all subsets of the set $\{a, b, c\}$, which is defined by the equation

$$f(x) = x \cup \{a, b\}. \tag{5.9}$$

Table 5.1 shows the values of $f(x)$ for all values of x. It is clear that this function has two fixpoints.

If a propositional program Π satisfies condition (α) then its reduct relative to any interpretation is a definite program (Sect. 4.3), so that it has a unique minimal model. We define the *stability operator* of Π as the function that maps every interpretation I to the minimal model of the reduct of I relative to Π. It is clear that the stable models of a program with property (α) can be characterized as the fixpoints of its stability operator.

Table 5.2, for instance, shows the values of the stability operator of program (5.5) and its fixpoints—the stable models of the program.

Exercise 5.5 For each of the given one-rule programs, make the table of values of its stability operator and mark its fixpoints.

(a) $q \leftarrow \neg p$,

(b) $p \leftarrow \neg\neg p$.

Exercise 5.6 Describe the stability operator of program (4.2)–(4.5) on page 57.

Table 5.1 Fixpoints of function (5.9)

x	$f(x)$	Fixpoint?
$\emptyset$	$\{a, b\}$	
$\{a\}$	$\{a, b\}$	
$\{b\}$	$\{a, b\}$	
$\{c\}$	$\{a, b, c\}$	
$\{a, b\}$	$\{a, b\}$	✓
$\{a, c\}$	$\{a, b, c\}$	
$\{b, c\}$	$\{a, b, c\}$	
$\{a, b, c\}$	$\{a, b.c\}$	✓

Table 5.2 Fixpoints of the stability operator s of program (5.5)

I	Reduct relative to I	$s(I)$	Fixpoint?
$\emptyset$	$\{p \leftarrow \top,\ q \leftarrow \top,\ r \leftarrow p,\ r \leftarrow q\}$	$\{p, q, r\}$	
$\{p\}$	$\{p \leftarrow \top,\ q \leftarrow \bot,\ r \leftarrow p,\ r \leftarrow q\}$	$\{p, r\}$	
$\{q\}$	$\{p \leftarrow \bot,\ q \leftarrow \top,\ r \leftarrow p,\ r \leftarrow q\}$	$\{q, r\}$	
$\{r\}$	$\{p \leftarrow \top,\ q \leftarrow \top,\ r \leftarrow p,\ r \leftarrow q\}$	$\{p, q, r\}$	
$\{p, q\}$	$\{p \leftarrow \bot,\ q \leftarrow \bot,\ r \leftarrow p,\ r \leftarrow q\}$	$\emptyset$	
$\{p, r\}$	$\{p \leftarrow \top,\ q \leftarrow \bot,\ r \leftarrow p,\ r \leftarrow q\}$	$\{p, r\}$	✓
$\{q, r\}$	$\{p \leftarrow \bot,\ q \leftarrow \top,\ r \leftarrow p,\ r \leftarrow q\}$	$\{q, r\}$	✓
$\{p, q, r\}$	$\{p \leftarrow \bot,\ q \leftarrow \bot,\ r \leftarrow p,\ r \leftarrow q\}$	$\emptyset$	

5.4   Simplifying Propositional Programs

Calculating stable models of a propositional program can be often facilitated by
simplifying it—by replacing it with a simpler program that has the same stable
models. In some cases, the simplified program will be in the class of positive
programs discussed in Chap. 4, and there will be no need to use the definition of
stable models in terms of reducts given in this chapter.

In Sect. 4.2 we talked about simplifying a set of propositional formulas in the
sense of replacing it by a simpler set of formulas that has the same models. When
we are interested in calculating stable models, it is important to keep in mind that
two propositional programs may have the same set of models but different sets of
stable models. Consider, for instance, three one-rule programs:

$$p \vee q, \qquad p \leftarrow \neg q, \qquad q \leftarrow \neg p.$$

These formulas are equivalent to each other, but their stable models are not the
same. The first rule is positive, and its stable models are its minimal models $\{p\}$
and $\{q\}$. The second has one stable model, $\{p\}$; the third has one stable model, $\{q\}$
(see Exercise 5.5 (a)).

For another example of equivalent programs with different stable models,
consider rule (5.7). It has two stable models, $\emptyset$ and $\{p\}$ (Exercise 5.5 (b)), but the
positive rule $p \leftarrow p$ obtained from it by dropping the pair of symbols $\neg\neg$ has only
one stable model—the minimal model $\emptyset$. Dropping a double negation is, of course,
an equivalent transformation, but it is not an acceptable simplification when our goal
is to find the stable models of a program.

Formula (5.7), known in logic as *the law of double negation*, is an example
of tautology that cannot be disregarded when we are interested in stable models:
dropping rule (5.7) from a propositional program, generally, changes its stable
models.

The input language of CLINGO allows us to write two negations in a row (which
is sometimes useful, as we will see in Sect. 8.4), and rule (5.7) can be written in that
language as

```
p :- not not p.
```

In response to this input, CLINGO generates two answers, in accordance with the
definition of a stable model above.

(The designers of CLINGO decided not to allow more than two negations in a
row, on the other hand. There is a good reason for that, as we will see in Sect. 6.1.)

Fortunately, many equivalent transformations are known to preserve the set of
stable models, so that they can be safely used for simplifying programs. Such
transformations are called "strongly" equivalent, and they are discussed in Sect. 6.1.

For the time being, it is sufficient for us to remember that the stable models of a program are preserved by the simplifications sanctioned by Table 4.1 on page 54.

In Sect. 4.2 we observed that a set of formulas containing an atomic formula p can be simplified by replacing p with $\top$ in the other formulas that contain p. The theorem below shows that this transformation preserves the collection of stable models. This is often useful, because many programs contain "facts," atomic formulas included in them as rules.

If Π is a propositional program and A is a set of atomic formulas, by $\Pi_{\top}^{A}$ we denote the propositional program obtained from Π by replacing all occurrences of formulas from A by $\top$.

Theorem on Facts *For any propositional program Π and any set A of atomic formulas, the program $\Pi \cup A$ has the same stable models as $\Pi_{\top}^{A} \cup A$.*

Theorem on Facts shows, for instance, that program (5.1) on page (71) has the same stable models as

$$p,$$
$$q,$$
$$r \leftarrow \top \wedge \neg s,$$
$$s \leftarrow \top$$

(take $A = \{p, q\}$, and include the last two rules of (5.1) in Π). Simplification steps from Table 4.1 turn this program into

$$p,$$
$$q,$$
$$r \leftarrow \neg s,$$
$$s.$$

Another application of Theorem on Facts gives

$$p,$$
$$q,$$
$$r \leftarrow \neg \top,$$
$$s.$$

Using Table 4.1 again, we replace the third rule by $r \leftarrow \bot$, then by $\top$, and then drop it altogether. The result is the program consisting of three atomic propositions p, q, s; its stable model is the minimal model $\{p, q, s\}$. We have found the stable model of program (5.1) without examining its reducts.

Exercise 5.7 Use Theorem on Facts to find all stable models of the given programs.

(a)

$$p,$$
$$q \leftarrow p,$$
$$r \leftarrow \neg q.$$

(b)

$$p,$$
$$q \vee r \leftarrow p,$$
$$s \vee t \leftarrow \neg p.$$

About an atomic formula we say that it is *irrelevant* for a propositional program Π if all its occurrences in Π are in the bodies of rules. The theorem below shows how irrelevant formulas can be removed without changing the stable models of the program. By $\Pi_{\perp}^{A}$ we denote the program obtained from Π by replacing all occurrences of atomic formulas from A by $\perp$.

Theorem on Irrelevant Formulas *For any set A of atomic formulas that are irrelevant for a propositional program Π, the programs Π and $\Pi_{\perp}^{A}$ have the same stable models.*

For example, r is irrelevant for the program

$$p \leftarrow \neg q,$$
$$q \leftarrow \neg r. \tag{5.10}$$

By Theorem on Irrelevant Formulas, this program can be rewritten as

$$p \leftarrow \neg q,$$
$$q \leftarrow \neg \perp$$

without changing its stable models. Using Table 4.1 and Theorem on Facts, we can further transform it into the atomic formula q. It follows that $\{q\}$ is the only stable model of (5.10).

Exercise 5.8 Use Theorem on Irrelevant Formulas to find the stable models of

(a) the program from Exercise 5.1;
(b) the program

$$p \leftarrow \neg q,$$
$$q \leftarrow \neg p \wedge r.$$

5.5   CLINGO **Programs with Negation**

The definition of the propositional image in Sects. 4.5 and 4.7 applies to CLINGO programs that consist of rules of forms (4.6) and (4.7), where each H_i and B_j is an atom or a comparison. To extend that definition to the case when H_i and B_j can be negated atoms, we need to extend Table 4.4 by lines showing how to form the propositional images of negated atoms. These additional lines are shown in Table 5.3. In this more general setting, the propositional image is a propositional program that may contain negation, and stable models of such programs are defined in Sect. 5.2. Thus we have now a precise definition of a stable model for sets of rules (4.6) and (4.7) in which every H_i and B_j is an atom, a comparison, or an atom prefixed with one or two negations.

Exercise 5.9   Find the propositional images of the rules

(a) `q :- (5/0).`
(b) `q :- not p(5/0).`
(c) `q :- not not p(5/0).`
(d) `(5/0) :- q.`
(e) `not p(5/0) :- q.`
(f) `not not p(5/0) :- q.`

Let us calculate, for example, the stable model of the CLINGO program

$$
\begin{aligned}
&p(a).\\
&q(a).\\
&r(X) \; :- \; p(X), \; not \; q(X).
\end{aligned}
\tag{5.11}
$$

Its propositional image is

$$
\begin{aligned}
&p(a),\\
&q(a),\\
&r(v) \leftarrow p(v) \wedge \neg q(v) \qquad \text{for all } v \text{ in } \mathbf{S} \cup \mathbf{Z}.
\end{aligned}
\tag{5.12}
$$

Table 5.3 Propositional images of negated ground atoms

Expression	Propositional image
`not` $p(t_1, \ldots, t_k)$ in the head	Conjunction of all formulas of the form $\neg p(v_1, \ldots, v_k)$ where v_i is a value of t_i ($i = 1, \ldots, k$)
`not` $p(t_1, \ldots, t_k)$ in the body	Disjunction of all formulas of the form $\neg p(v_1, \ldots, v_k)$ where v_i is a value of t_i ($i = 1, \ldots, k$)
`not not` $p(t_1, \ldots, t_k)$ in the head	Conjunction of all formulas of the form $\neg\neg p(v_1, \ldots, v_k)$ where v_i is a value of t_i ($i = 1, \ldots, k$)
`not not` $p(t_1, \ldots, t_k)$ in the body	Disjunction of all formulas of the form $\neg\neg p(v_1, \ldots, v_k)$ where v_i is a value of t_i ($i = 1, \ldots, k$)

For all v other than a, $p(v)$ does not occur in the heads of these rules. By Theorem on Irrelevant Formulas, it follows that all rules in the last line with v different from a can be dropped, and the propositional image can be rewritten as the finite program

$$p(a),$$
$$q(a),$$
$$r(a) \leftarrow p(a) \wedge \neg q(a).$$

By Theorem on Facts, it can be further rewritten as

$$p(a),$$
$$q(a),$$
$$r(a) \leftarrow \top \wedge \neg \top,$$

and then the last rule can be dropped. The only stable model of (5.11) is $\{p(a), q(a)\}$.

Consider now a modification of program (5.11) in which both occurrences of a are replaced by intervals:

```
p(1..3).
q(3..5).                                    (5.13)
r(X) :- p(X), not q(X).
```

The propositional image of this program, simplified using the fact that the atoms $p(v)$ with v different from $1, 2, 3$, are irrelevant for it, is

$$p(1) \wedge p(2) \wedge p(3),$$
$$q(3) \wedge q(4) \wedge q(5), \qquad\qquad (5.14)$$
$$r(n) \leftarrow p(n) \wedge \neg q(n) \qquad (n = 1, 2, 3).$$

Theorem on Facts is not directly applicable to this program. It is known, however, that if a rule is a conjunction then replacing it by the set of its conjunctive terms does not affect the stable models. It follows that program (5.14) has the same stable models as the program

$$p(1), \ p(2), \ p(3),$$
$$q(3), \ q(4), \ q(5),$$
$$r(n) \leftarrow p(n) \wedge \neg q(n) \qquad (n = 1, 2, 3).$$

Now Theorem on Facts can be used to transform this program into its stable model

$$\{p(1), p(2), p(3), q(3), q(4), q(5), r(1), r(2)\}.$$

These atoms form the only stable model of program (5.13).

As another example, let us calculate the stable model of the program consisting of rules (2.9) and (2.10) on page 16. Its propositional image consists of the rules

$$composite(4) \leftarrow \top \wedge \top \wedge \top,$$
$$prime(2) \leftarrow \top \wedge \neg composite(2),$$
$$prime(3) \leftarrow \top \wedge \neg composite(3),$$
$$prime(4) \leftarrow \top \wedge \neg composite(4),$$
$$prime(5) \leftarrow \top \wedge \neg composite(5)$$

and infinitely many propositional rules containing $\bot$ as a conjunctive term in the body. Simplification steps from Table 4.1 turn it into the finite program

$$composite(4),$$
$$prime(2) \leftarrow \neg composite(2),$$
$$prime(3) \leftarrow \neg composite(3), \tag{5.15}$$
$$prime(4) \leftarrow \neg composite(4),$$
$$prime(5) \leftarrow \neg composite(5).$$

Further simplifications using Theorem on Irrelevant Formulas and Theorem on Facts transform it into its stable model

$$\{prime(2), prime(3), composite(4), prime(5)\}.$$

Exercise 5.10 (a)   Find the propositional image of the program

```
p(5..7).
q(X) :- X = 1..5, not p(X).
```

(b)   Calculate its stable models.

Exercise 5.11 Do the same for the program

```
p(5..7).
q(X) :- p(X), not p(X+1).
```

5.6   The Law of Excluded Middle

The tautology

$$p \vee \neg p \tag{5.16}$$

is known in logic as *the law of excluded middle*. (Any proposition p is either true or false, there is nothing in the middle.) Like the law of double negation (page 73), it has two stable models, $\emptyset$ and $\{p\}$. Indeed, the reduct of (5.16) relative to $\emptyset$ is $p \vee \top$, which is equivalent to $\top$; the minimal model of the reduct is empty. The reduct of (5.16) relative to $\{p\}$ is $p \vee \bot$, which is equivalent to p; the minimal model of the reduct is $\{p\}$.

In rule (5.16), negation occurs in the head, and not in the body as in the examples that we have seen before. CLINGO does not object against negation in the head. It will accept program (5.16) if we rewrite it as

```
p, not p.
```

and it will produce two stable models for it, in accordance with the calculation above. In other words, CLINGO views this rule as synonymous to the choice rule $\{p\}$.

Exercise 5.12 (a) Find all stable models of the program

$$p \vee q,$$
$$\neg p \vee r.$$

(b) Check that the result of your calculation is in agreement with the output of CLINGO.

The law of excluded middle plays an important role in the theory of stable models because of its close relation to choice rules, and also because of the following fact:

Theorem on Excluded Middle *An interpretation I is a model of a propositional program Π if and only if I is a stable model of the program obtained from Π by adding the rules $p \vee \neg p$ for all atomic formulas p.*

For example, an interpretation I is a model of the propositional program from Exercise 4.3 (page 53) if and only if it is a stable model of the program obtained from it by adding the rules

$$p \vee \neg p, \; q \vee \neg q, \; r \vee \neg r.$$

That means that the question from Exercise 4.3 can be answered by running CLINGO on the program

```
p :- q, r.
q :- p.
r :- p.
{p}.
{q}.
(r}.
```

The last three lines can be abbreviated as

$$\{p; \; q; \; r\}.$$

Exercise 5.13 Use CLINGO to verify your answers to Exercises 4.3, 4.4, 4.5(a), 4.5(b), 4.13(a).

The next example of calculating stable models is related to the use of logic programs for representing games. We are given a finite directed acyclic graph G, such as the one shown in Fig. 5.1. A token is placed on one of the vertices, and two players take turns moving the token to other vertices along the edges of the graph. When the player who has to move finds the token on a vertex without outgoing edges, that player has lost. Whether the player who starts can win is determined by the vertex where the token was placed initially. For instance, in the graph shown in Fig. 5.1, vertices b and c are winning (move the token to d), and vertices a and d are not.

The set `winning/1` of winning vertices can be described by the CLINGO rule

$$\text{winning(X)} \ \text{:- edge(X,Y), not winning(Y).} \qquad (5.17)$$

(a vertex is winning if there is an edge leading from it to a vertex that is not winning). The set of winning vertices can be determined by running CLINGO on the program Π_G obtained by adding this rule to the definition of the predicate `edge/2` for graph G.

We would like to calculate the stable model of this program for the graph in Fig. 5.1. The propositional image of this program consists of the rules

$$edge(a, b), \ edge(b, c), \ edge(b, d), \ edge(c, d) \qquad (5.18)$$

and

$$winning(v_1) \leftarrow edge(v_1, v_2) \wedge \neg winning(v_2) \qquad (5.19)$$

for all v_1, v_2 in $\mathbf{S} \cup \mathbf{Z}$. Using Theorem on Irrelevant Formulas and Theorem on Facts, we can replace (5.19) by the rules corresponding to the edges of G:

$$winning(a) \leftarrow \neg winning(b),$$
$$winning(b) \leftarrow \neg winning(c),$$
$$winning(b) \leftarrow \neg winning(d),$$
$$winning(c) \leftarrow \neg winning(d).$$

Fig. 5.1 Acyclic directed graph

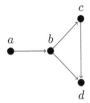

Since $winning(d)$ is irrelevant, these rules can be further rewritten as

$$winning(a) \leftarrow \neg winning(b),$$
$$winning(b) \leftarrow \neg winning(c),$$
$$winning(b),$$
$$winning(c),$$

and then, using again Theorem on Facts, as

$$winning(b), \ winning(c). \tag{5.20}$$

Consequently the only stable model of Π_G in this case consists of atoms (5.18) and (5.20).

5.7   CLINGO **Programs with Choice**

In this section, we extend the definition of propositional image to choice expressions

$$\{A_1; \dots; A_n\} \tag{5.21}$$

where each A_i is a ground atom. The special case when $m = 1$, and A_1 contains neither arithmetic operations nor intervals, is particularly simple. In this case, we take the formula

$$A_1 \vee \neg A_1$$

to be the propositional image of (5.21). This definition is motivated by the relationship between choice rules and the law of excluded middle discussed in Sect. 5.6.

For example, the propositional image of the program

```
{p(a)}.
q(X)  :- p(X).
```

is the propositional program

$$p(a) \vee \neg p(a),$$
$$q(v) \leftarrow p(v) \qquad (v \in \mathbf{S} \cup \mathbf{Z}). \tag{5.22}$$

To calculate its stable models, observe first that the atoms $p(v)$ with v different from a do not occur in the heads of its rules. It follows that the rules in the second line with v different from a can be dropped. To find the stable models of the remaining two rules

$$p(a) \vee \neg p(a),$$
$$q(a) \leftarrow p(a)$$

consider an arbitrary interpretation I. Case 1: $p(a) \in I$. The reduct is

$$p(a) \vee \bot,$$
$$q(a) \leftarrow p(a).$$

The first rule is equivalent to $p(a)$, so that the only minimal of the reduct is $\{p(a), q(a)\}$. Case 2: $p(a) \notin I$. The reduct is

$$p(a) \vee \top,$$
$$q(a) \leftarrow p(a).$$

The first rule is a tautology, so that the only minimal of the reduct is $\emptyset$. We conclude that the stable models of (5.22) are $\{p(a), q(a)\}$ and $\emptyset$.

Exercise 5.14 (a) Find the propositional image of the program

```
p(a).
{q(X)} :- p(X).
```

(b) Calculate its stable models.

Exercise 5.15 Do the same for the program

```
{p(X)}.
{q(X)} :- p(X).
```

Let us turn now to the more general case of a choice expression

$$\{ p(t_1, \ldots, t_k) \}$$

that may contain arithmetic operations and intervals. Its propositional image is defined as the conjunction of all formulas of the form

$$p(v_1, \ldots, v_k) \vee \neg p(v_1, \ldots, v_k)$$

where each v_i is a value of t_i ($i = 1, \ldots, k$). For instance, the propositional image of

$$\{ q(1..8, 1..8) \}$$

is the conjunction of the 64 formulas

$$q(i, j) \vee \neg q(i, j) \qquad (1 \le i, j \le 8).$$

The propositional image of

$$\{q(1..8,8..1)\}$$

is the empty conjunction $\top$.

Exercise 5.16 (a)   Find the propositional image of the program

```
p(0..1).
{q(5/X)}  :-  p(X).
```

(b)   Calculate its stable models.

Exercise 5.17 Do the same for the program

```
p(5).
{q(X,0..1)}  :-  p(X).
```

The propositional image of expression (5.21) with n greater than 1 is defined as the conjunction of the propositional images of the expressions $\{A_i\}$ for $i = 1, \ldots, n$. For example, the propositional image of

$$\{p(0);\ p(1)\}$$

is

$$(p(0) \vee \neg p(0)) \wedge (p(1) \vee \neg p(1))$$

—the same as that of $\{p(0..1)\}$.

5.8   Theorem on Constraints

Recall that a rule in the input language of CLINGO is called a constraint if its head is empty (Sect. 2.7). By adding a constraint to a CLINGO program we eliminate its stable models that violate the constraint. This useful observation is somewhat vague, because we have not defined the precise meaning of "violate."

In the world of propositional programs, a *constraint* is a propositional rule of the form $\bot \leftarrow F$. The propositional image of a CLINGO constraint, as defined in Sects. 4.5, 4.7, is a constraint in the sense of this definition, because the empty disjunction is $\bot$ (Sect. 4.2).

The vague observation on the effect of constraints on the behavior of CLINGO turns, in the world of propositional programs, into a theorem:

Theorem on Constraints *Let Π be a propositional program, and let Σ be a set of constraints. An interpretation I is a stable model of $\Pi \cup \Sigma$ if and only if I is a stable model of Π and a model of Σ.*

This theorem shows, for instance, that an interpretation I is a stable model of the program from Exercise 5.3 if and only if it is a stable model of its first rule that does not satisfy the body $p \wedge \neg q$ of the constraint. The first rule is positive, and its stable models are its minimal models $\{p\}$, $\{q\}$. The first of them satisfies $p \wedge \neg q$, and the second does not. We can conclude that $\{q\}$ is the only stable model of the program.

Exercise 5.18 (a) Use Theorem on Constraints to find the stable models of the program

$$p \vee q,$$
$$r \leftarrow p,$$
$$s \leftarrow q,$$
$$\bot \leftarrow \neg p,$$
$$\bot \leftarrow \neg r \wedge \neg s.$$

(b) Check that your answer is in agreement with the output of CLINGO.

Exercise 5.19 Find the stable models of the program

```
p(5).
{q(X,0..1)} :- p(X).
:- not q(5,0).
```

5.9 Bibliographical and Historical Remarks

Stable models can be characterized in many different ways [79]. They were originally defined for rules of the form

$$A_0 \leftarrow A_1 \wedge \cdots \wedge A_m \wedge \neg A_{m+1} \wedge \cdots \wedge \neg A_n, \tag{5.23}$$

where each A_i is an atomic formula [40, 51]. The expression "self-verifying" was introduced in the first of these papers, and the term "stable model" in the second. But using the idea of a self-verifying conjecture to describe nonmonotonic reasoning is older than the definition of a stable model. We find it, in particular, in the definitions of default logic [107] and autoepistemic logic [96]. Default logic is an extension of first-order logic in which the set of postulates is allowed to contain *defaults*— postulates of the form

$$\frac{F \; : \; MG_1, \ldots, MG_n}{H}. \tag{5.24}$$

Formula F is the *premise* of the default, formulas $G_1, \ldots, G_n$ are its *justifications*, and formula H is its *conclusion*. The symbol M is read as "it is consistent to assume", and default (5.24) is understood, informally speaking, as permission to derive the conclusion from the premise if the justifications can be consistently assumed. The semantics of defaults is made precise using a fixpoint construction similar to the one presented in Sect. 5.3. A propositional rule of form (5.23) can be viewed [13] as alternative notation for the default

$$\frac{A_1 \wedge \cdots \wedge A_m \; : \mathsf{M} \neg A_{m+1}, \ldots, \mathsf{M} \neg A_n}{A_0}.$$

Autoepistemic logic is another nonmonotonic logic closely related to stable models. Its formulas may contain, in addition to propositional connectives, the logical operator L. The formula $\mathsf{L}\, F$ is read "F is believed," and the precise meaning of this operator is defined in terms of fixpoints. The autoepistemic counterpart of rule (5.23) is

$$A_0 \leftarrow A_1 \wedge \cdots \wedge A_m \wedge \neg\mathsf{L}\, A_{m+1} \wedge \cdots \wedge \neg\mathsf{L}\, A_n.$$

From this perspective, negation as failure in logic programming has the same meaning as the combination $\neg\mathsf{L}$ in autoepistemic logic [48].

The original definition of a stable model was extended to rules with disjunctions in the head [53], and then to rules in which conjunction, disjunction, and negation can be nested arbitrarily in heads and bodies [83], as in propositional rules in the sense of Sect. 4.1. The original definition of a stable model for programs with choice rules [99] treated choice as an independent construct; a few years later it became clear that $\{\mathrm{p}\}$ can be viewed also as shorthand for the combination $\mathrm{p, not\ p}$ [38].

The definition of the propositional image of a choice expression in Sect. 5.7 is restricted to expressions (5.21) without bounds on cardinality and without local variables. Overcoming the first limitation is not difficult, because cardinality bounds can be replaced by constraints (Sect. 2.7). For example, the propositional image of a ground rule of the form

$$1 \; \{A_1; \ldots; A_n\}.$$

that contains neither arithmetic operations nor intervals can be defined as the set of $n + 1$ propositional rules

$$
\begin{aligned}
&A_i \vee \neg A_i \qquad (i = 1, \ldots, n), \\
&\bot \leftarrow \neg A_1 \wedge \cdots \wedge \neg A_n.
\end{aligned}
$$

Extending this idea to rules with local variables is more difficult. One approach to this problem is to use formulas that may contain infinite conjunctions and disjunctions, such as

$$q \leftarrow p_1 \wedge p_2 \wedge \ldots \quad \text{and} \quad q \leftarrow p_1 \vee p_2 \vee \ldots .$$

Infinitary formulas have been studied in logic since the 1950s [68, 111]. They can be denoted by expressions containing the "big conjunction" and "big disjunction" symbols, similar to the symbol $\sum$ used in algebra to represent the sum of a set of numbers:

$$q \leftarrow \bigwedge_{n \geq 1} p_n, \quad q \leftarrow \bigvee_{n \geq 1} p_n. \tag{5.25}$$

In some cases, an infinitary propositional formula has the same meaning as a set of finite formulas. For instance, the second of formulas (5.25) is equivalent to the infinite set of finite implications

$$q \leftarrow p_1, \, q \leftarrow p_2, \, \ldots .$$

But the first of formulas (5.25) is not equivalent to any set of finite propositional formulas.

The definition of a stable model can be extended to rules with infinitary heads and bodies [116], and this generalization can be used to define the propositional image of a choice rule with local variables [44]. For example, the rule

$$1 \; \{q(X) \; : \; p(X)\}. \tag{5.26}$$

can be represented by the combination of the propositional rules

$$q(v) \vee \neg q(v) \leftarrow p(v)$$

for all v in $\mathbf{S} \cup \mathbf{Z}$ with the infinitary constraint that does not allow the set q to be disjoint from p:

$$\bot \leftarrow \bigwedge_{v \in \mathbf{S} \cup \mathbf{Z}} \neg(p(v) \wedge q(v)).$$

Theorem on Facts is a special case of splitting—dividing the rules of the program into two parts, calculating the stable models of one part, and then extending each of them to find the stable models of the entire program [84]. Splitting can be applied, for instance, to program (5.5) on page 72. The part consisting of the first two rules of the program has two stable models, $\{p\}$ and $\{q\}$; the last two rules turn $\{p\}$ into $\{p, r\}$, and $\{q\}$ into $\{q, r\}$. Theorem on Irrelevant Formulas can be viewed as a special case of splitting as well.

The encoding of two-person games in Sect. 5.5 is similar to an encoding written originally for Prolog [118].

Chapter 6
Mathematics of Stable Models

In Chap. 5 we saw how properties of stable models expressed by Theorem on Facts, Theorem on Irrelevant Formulas, and Theorem on Constraints can be used sometimes to calculate the stable models of a program without referring to the definition of a stable model directly. This chapter discusses other useful properties of stable models.

6.1 Strong Equivalence

We start by examining more closely the class of equivalent transformations that do not affect the stable models of a propositional program.

Definition About sets Π_1, Π_2 of propositional rules we say that they are *strongly equivalent* to each other if, for every propositional program Π, the program $\Pi \cup \Pi_1$ has the same stable models as $\Pi \cup \Pi_2$.

This definition says essentially that replacing a group of rules within a propositional program by a strongly equivalent group of rules does not affect the set of stable models of the program. For example, in Sect. 5.5 we claimed that if one of the rules of a propositional program is a conjunction then replacing it by the set of its conjunctive terms does not affect the stable models of the program. That claim can be expressed by saying that a rule of the form

$$F_1 \wedge \cdots \wedge F_n \tag{6.1}$$

is strongly equivalent to the set of n rules

$$F_1, \ldots, F_n. \tag{6.2}$$

© Springer Nature Switzerland AG 2019
V. Lifschitz, *Answer Set Programming*,
https://doi.org/10.1007/978-3-030-24658-7_6

The observation in Sect. 5.4 that the equivalent one-rule programs

$$p \vee \neg\neg p \text{ and } p \leftarrow p$$

have different sets of stable models shows that these rules are not strongly equivalent to each other. In this case we do not even need to combine the two rules with any additional rules to see that they are not strongly equivalent. In other words, the empty set Π can serve in this case as a counterexample. The same can be said about the rules

$$p \vee q, \qquad p \leftarrow \neg q, \qquad q \leftarrow \neg p. \tag{6.3}$$

Their sets of stable models are different from each other; there is no need to add any rules Π to them to show that they are not strongly equivalent. On the other hand, the first of rules (6.3) has the same stable models as the program consisting of the last two rules (Sect. 5.2), but it is not strongly equivalent to that program. Indeed, adding the rules

$$\begin{aligned} p &\leftarrow q, \\ q &\leftarrow p \end{aligned} \tag{6.4}$$

to the rule $p \vee q$ gives a program with the stable model $\{p, q\}$, but adding the same rules to

$$\begin{aligned} p &\leftarrow \neg q, \\ q &\leftarrow \neg p \end{aligned}$$

gives a program without stable models (Exercise 5.4 on page 75). In this case, rules (6.4) play the role of Π.

Exercise 6.1 Prove that $\neg\neg p$ is not strongly equivalent to p.

Exercise 6.2 Prove that $\neg q \leftarrow \neg p$ is not strongly equivalent to $p \leftarrow q$.

The use of the term "*strongly* equivalent" is justified by the fact that any two sets of propositional rules that are strongly equivalent to each other are also equivalent— that is, have the same models. To prove this assertion, assume that Π_1 is strongly equivalent to Π_2, and take Π to be the set of the excluded middle formulas $p \vee \neg p$ for all atomic formulas p. Then $\Pi \cup \Pi_1$ and $\Pi \cup \Pi_2$ have the same stable models. But by Theorem on Excluded Middle, the set of stable models of $\Pi \cup \Pi_1$ is the set of all models of Π_1, and the set of stable models of $\Pi \cup \Pi_2$ is the set of all models of Π_2. It follows that Π_1 and Π_2 have the same models.

When our goal is to prove that two programs Π_1 and Π_2 are not strongly equivalent to each other, we look for a counterexample—a program Π such that one of the programs $\Pi \cup \Pi_1$, $\Pi \cup \Pi_2$ has a stable model that is not a stable model of the other. But when we want to prove that two programs are strongly equivalent, how can this be done?

We can assert that propositional programs Π_1 and Π_2 are strongly equivalent to each other whenever we can show that the reduct of Π_1 relative to any interpretation is equivalent to the reduct of Π_2 relative to the same interpretation. Indeed, let Π', Π'_1, and Π'_2 be the reducts of programs Π, Π_1, and Π_2, respectively, relative to the same interpretation I. Whether I is a stable model of $\Pi \cup \Pi_i$ ($i = 1, 2$) is completely determined by the set of all models of $\Pi' \cup \Pi'_i$. But if Π'_1 and Π'_2 are equivalent to each other then $\Pi' \cup \Pi'_1$ and $\Pi' \cup \Pi'_2$ are equivalent to each other as well.

For example, this reasoning can be used to prove that (6.1) is strongly equivalent to (6.2). Indeed, if the reduct of (6.2) relative to some interpretation I is

$$F'_1, \ldots, F'_n \tag{6.5}$$

then the reduct of (6.2) relative to I is

$$F'_1 \wedge \cdots \wedge F'_n. \tag{6.6}$$

It is clear that (6.6) is equivalent to (6.5).

In a similar way, we can check that any rule of the form $F \leftarrow G \wedge \top$ is strongly equivalent to $F \leftarrow G$. Indeed, the reducts of these rules relative to the same interpretation are the equivalent formulas $F' \leftarrow G' \wedge \top$ and $F' \leftarrow G'$.

For most other transformations sanctioned by Table 4.1, the claim that they are strongly equivalent can be established in a similar way.

Exercise 6.3 Prove that if two sets of positive propositional rules are equivalent to each other then they are strongly equivalent.

Let us check now that $\neg\neg\neg F$ is strongly equivalent to $\neg F$. Consider any interpretation I. The reduct of each of the two formulas relative to an interpretation I is $\bot$ if I satisfies F, and $\top$ otherwise. In either case, both formulas have the same reduct.

A similar calculation shows that $G \leftarrow \neg\neg\neg F$ is strongly equivalent to $G \leftarrow \neg F$. More generally, removing two of three successive negations anywhere within a propositional rule is a strongly equivalent transformation. This is why allowing more than two negations in a row within a CLINGO rule would be pointless.

In Sect. 2.7 we claimed that replacing the CLINGO constraint

```
:- f(X,Y1), f(X,Y2), Y1! = Y2.
```

by the rule

```
Y1 = Y2 :- f(X,Y1), f(X,Y2).
```

does not affect the stable models of a program. More generally, replacing a constraint of the form

$$:-\ \ldots,\ t_1\ != t_2\ .\tag{6.7}$$

by

$$t_1\ =\ t_2\ :-\ \ldots.\tag{6.8}$$

within any CLINGO program does not affect its stable models. To see why, note that the propositional image of a ground rule of form (6.7) has the form

$$\bot \leftarrow F \wedge \bot$$

if the set of values of t_1 is the same as the set of values of t_2, and

$$\bot \leftarrow F \wedge \top$$

otherwise. The propositional image of (6.8) is

$$\top \leftarrow F$$

or

$$\bot \leftarrow F$$

depending on the same condition. In either case, the propositional images are strongly equivalent to each other.

Exercise 6.4 Replacing a rule of the form

$$\ldots\ :-\ t_1\ != t_2\ .\tag{6.9}$$

by

$$\ldots,\ t_1\ =\ t_2\ .\tag{6.10}$$

within any CLINGO program does not affect its stable models. True or false?

In Sect. 5.6 we observed that the rule $p \leftarrow \neg\neg p$ has the same stable models as $p \vee \neg p$. In fact, these two rules are strongly equivalent to each other. More generally, any rule of the form $F \leftarrow \neg\neg F$ is strongly equivalent to $F \vee \neg F$. Indeed, if the reduct of the former relative to some interpretation is $F' \leftarrow \top$ then the reduct of the latter relative to the same interpretation is $F' \vee \bot$; if the reduct of the former is $F' \leftarrow \bot$ then the reduct of the latter is $F' \vee \top$. Either way, the two reducts are equivalent to each other.

Exercise 6.5 Any rule of the form

$$F \leftarrow \neg\neg F \wedge G \tag{6.11}$$

is strongly equivalent to

$$F \vee \neg F \leftarrow G. \tag{6.12}$$

True or false?

There are cases when two rules are strongly equivalent, but this cannot be established by the method used in the examples above. For instance, the rules

$$\bot \leftarrow F \text{ and } \neg F \tag{6.13}$$

are strongly equivalent to each other (this is one of the simplifications from Table 4.1). But the reduct of the former, if F is an atom (or any formula that does not contain negation), is $\bot \leftarrow F$; the reduct of the latter is $\top$ or $\bot$.

The fact that rules (6.13) are strongly equivalent can be derived from Theorem on Constraints (Sect. 5.8), as follows. We need to show that for any propositional program Π, an interpretation I is a stable model of $\Pi \cup \{\bot \leftarrow F\}$ if and only if it is a stable model of $\Pi \cup \{\neg F\}$. Let Π' be the reduct of Π relative to I. The reduct of $\Pi \cup \{\neg F\}$ relative to I is

$\Pi' \cup \{\bot\}$, which is equivalent to $\bot$, if I satisfies F, and
$\Pi' \cup \{\top\}$, which is equivalent to Π', otherwise.

Consequently I is a minimal model of this reduct if and only if I does not satisfy F and is a minimal model of Π'. By Theorem on Constraints, this condition is satisfied if and only if I is a stable model of Π.

A propositional rule is *strongly tautological* if it is strongly equivalent to the empty program. Thus the set of stable models of a program does not change when a strongly tautological rule is added or removed.

We can assert that a propositional rule is strongly tautological if we can show that all its reducts are tautologies. For instance, any rule of the form $F \leftarrow G \wedge \bot$ is strongly tautological, because its reducts have the form $F' \leftarrow G' \wedge \bot$ and consequently are tautologies.

If a positive rule is a tautology then it is strongly tautological. This fact follows from the assertion of Exercise 6.3.

Exercise 6.6 For each of the given expressions, determine whether every propositional rule of this form is strongly tautological.

(a) $F \vee \neg F$,
(b) $\neg F \vee \neg\neg F$,
(c) $\bot \leftarrow F \wedge \neg F$,
(d) $F \leftarrow F \wedge G$,
(e) $F \vee G \leftarrow F$.

6.2 Theorem on Strong Equivalence

Is there an algorithm that decides, for any two finite sets of propositional rules, whether they are strongly equivalent to each other?

If we ask this question about equivalence (as defined in Sect. 4.2), rather than strong equivalence, then the answer will be obviously yes: we can list, in principle, all possible assignments of truth values to the atomic formulas occurring in the rules, and check if any of them is a model of one set of rules but not a model of the other. As to strong equivalence, it is not immediately clear how to recognize it in a finite number of steps, because the definition of strong equivalence talks about arbitrary propositional programs, and there are infinitely many of them.

It turns out that strong equivalence can be verified using a process that is similar to the one described above, except that it uses three truth values, instead of two. These truth values will be represented by numbers 0, 1/2, and 1. We can think of 0 as falsity, and the other two truth values as representing two different degrees of truth. Distinguishing between two positive truth values as described below is referred to as the use of "the logic of here-and-there."

If one of three truth values is assigned to every atomic formula then the values of other formulas are calculated according to the following rules:

1. The value of $\perp$ is 0, and the value of $\top$ is 1.
2. The value of $\neg F$ is 1 if the value of F is 0, and it is 0 otherwise.
3. The value of $F \wedge G$ is the minimum of the values of F and G.
4. The value of $F \vee G$ is the maximum of the values of F and G.
5. If the value of F is x, and the value of G is y, then the value of $F \leftarrow G$ is 1 if $x \geq y$, and x otherwise.

If a formula F gets the same truth value as a formula G for every assignment of truth values 0, 1/2, 1 to atomic formulas then we say that F *is equivalent to G in the logic of here-and-there.*

Table 6.1 shows the calculation of truth values for several formulas. We see that, in the logic of here-and-there, p is not equivalent to $\neg\neg p$, but

- $\neg p$ is equivalent to $\neg\neg\neg p$,
- $p \vee \neg p$ is equivalent to $p \leftarrow \neg\neg p$,
- $\perp \leftarrow p$ is equivalent to $\neg p$.

These facts match the observations about strong equivalence made in the previous section. This is not an accident:

Table 6.1 Calculating truth values in the logic of here-and-there

p	$\neg p$	$\neg\neg p$	$\neg\neg\neg p$	$p \vee \neg p$	$\perp \leftarrow p$	$p \leftarrow \neg\neg p$
0	1	0	1	1	1	1
1/2	0	1	0	1/2	0	1/2
1	0	1	0	1	0	1

Table 6.2 The formulas in the last two columns are not equivalent in the logic of here-and-there

p	q	$\neg q$	$p \leftarrow \neg q$	$\neg p$	$q \leftarrow \neg p$	$(p \leftarrow \neg q) \wedge (q \leftarrow \neg p)$	$p \vee q$
1/2	1/2	0	1	0	1	1	1/2

Theorem on Strong Equivalence *Finite sets Π_1, Π_2 of propositional rules are strongly equivalent to each other if and only if the conjunction of rules Π_1 is equivalent to the conjunction of rules Π_2 in the logic of here-and-there.*

According to this theorem, the question whether two sets of propositional rules formed from n atomic formulas are strongly equivalent to each other can be resolved by examining the truth values of these rules in the logic of here-and-there for all 3^n assignments of truth values 0, 1/2, 1 to atomic formulas. When we want to prove that sets Π_1, Π_2 of rules are not strongly equivalent, there is no need now to look for a program Π such that $\Pi \cup \Pi_1$ and $\Pi \cup \Pi_2$ have different stable models; instead, we can provide a counterexample of a different kind: a line in the three-valued truth table in which the value of Π_1 is is different from the value of Π_2.

For example, we showed earlier that the first of rules (6.3) is not strongly equivalent to the combination of the last two rules using the additional rules (6.4) as a counterexample. An alternative way to prove that assertion is to calculate the truth values of rules (6.3) when the value 1/2 is assigned to both p and q (Table 6.2).

Exercise 6.7 Prove that the propositional program

$$q \leftarrow p,$$
$$q \leftarrow \neg p$$

is not strongly equivalent to q in two ways: (a) directly, using the definition of strong equivalence, and (b) using the logic of here-and-there.

In the special case when Π_1 is a single rule and Π_2 is empty, Theorem on Strong Equivalence shows that a rule is strongly tautological if and only if it gets the value 1 every assignment of truth values 0, 1/2, 1 to atomic formulas. For example, to show that the rule from Exercise 6.6 (e) is strongly tautological we only need to observe that $\max(x, y) \geq x$.

6.3 Program Completion

The task of finding a stable model of a propositional program can be sometimes reduced to the task of finding *any* model of a certain set of propositional formulas. The latter task is often easier, because arbitrary equivalent transformations can be used in the process, not only strongly equivalent.

This reduction is accomplished by forming the *completion* of the program. Completion is defined for propositional programs satisfying condition (α) from

Sect. 5.3 (which says that the heads of all rules are atomic formulas) and the condition

(β) for every atomic formula p, the set of rules of the program with the head p is finite.

This additional condition is trivially satisfied if the program has finitely many rules. But there are also infinite programs with property (β). For instance, the propositional image of the CLINGO rule

$$q(X) \; :- \; p(X).$$

consists of infinitely many propositional rules

$$q(v) \leftarrow p(v) \qquad (v \in \mathbf{S} \cup \mathbf{Z}),$$

but every atom $q(v)$ is the head of only one of these rules. On the other hand, condition (β) is violated for the propositional image of the rule

$$q(X) \; :- \; p(X,Y). \tag{6.14}$$

It consists of the rules

$$q(v_1) \leftarrow p(v_1, v_2) \qquad (v_1, v_2 \in \mathbf{S} \cup \mathbf{Z}), \tag{6.15}$$

and every atom of the form $q(v)$ is the head of infinitely many of them.

Let Π be a propositional program satisfying conditions (α) and (β). For every atomic formula p from the vocabulary of Π, by B_p we denote

- formula $\top$, if p is one of the rules of Π,
- the disjunction of the bodies of all rules of Π with the head p, otherwise.

(Condition (β) guarantees that this disjunction is finite.)

Definition The *completion* of a propositional program Π satisfying conditions (α) and (β) is the set of formulas

$$p \leftrightarrow B_p \tag{6.16}$$

for all atomic formulas p.

Consider, for instance, program (5.1) on page 71 and assume that the vocabulary (the set of all atomic formulas) is $\{p, q, r, s\}$. The completion of the program consists of the formulas

$$
\begin{aligned}
p &\leftrightarrow \top, \\
q &\leftrightarrow \top, \\
r &\leftrightarrow p \wedge \neg s, \\
s &\leftrightarrow q.
\end{aligned}
\tag{6.17}
$$

If the vocabulary includes any atomic formulas other than p, q, r, s, then the completion will include also the formulas

$$
x \leftrightarrow \bot
$$

for every such atomic formula x. (Recall that the disjunction of the empty set is $\bot$.)

In the examples and exercises in the rest of this section we assume that the vocabulary includes only the atomic formulas that occur in the given program.

The completion of program (5.5) on page 72 is

$$
\begin{aligned}
p &\leftrightarrow \neg q, \\
q &\leftrightarrow \neg p, \\
r &\leftrightarrow p \vee q.
\end{aligned}
\tag{6.18}
$$

The intuition behind the concept of completion is that the bodies of rules with the head p can be viewed as sufficient conditions for the validity of p, and formula (6.16) says that, collectively, these sufficient conditions are also necessary. For instance, the last two rules of program (5.5) tell us that p is a sufficient condition for r, and so is q; the last of formulas (6.18) says that r is true if *and only if* at least one of these sufficient conditions holds. It says, in other words, that the disjunction of these sufficient conditions is necessary and sufficient.

In many cases, the set of stable models of a propositional program is exactly the same as the set of all models of its completion. As an example, let us find all models of the completion (6.17) of program (5.1). Equivalent transformations turn the completion into

$$
\begin{aligned}
&p, \\
&q, \\
&r \leftrightarrow \neg s, \\
&s.
\end{aligned}
$$

It is clear that these formulas have one model, $\{p, q, s\}$. As we know, this is the only stable model of program (5.1).

Consider now the completion (6.18) of program (5.5). To simplify it, note that the first of formulas (6.18) allows us to replace p by $\neg q$ in the other two formulas:

$$p \leftrightarrow \neg q,$$
$$q \leftrightarrow \neg\neg q,$$
$$r \leftrightarrow \neg q \vee q.$$

This set of formulas is equivalent to

$$p \leftrightarrow \neg q,$$
$$r.$$

It follows that (6.18) has two models, corresponding to two ways to assign a truth value to q: $\{p, r\}$ (q is false) and $\{q, r\}$ (q is true). As in the other examples, the set of all models of the program's completion coincides with the set of stable models.

For one more example, consider the completion

$$p \leftrightarrow \neg\neg p$$

of program (5.7) on page 73. It is a tautology, and its two models $\emptyset$ and $\{p\}$ are the stable models of the program.

Exercise 6.8

(a) Form the completion of the program from Exercise 5.1 on page 73.
(b) Check that the stable model of that program is the only stable model of its completion.

There are cases, however, when the set of stable models of a program and the set of all models of its completion differ from each other. The simplest example is given by the program

$$p \leftarrow p.$$

It is definite, and its only stable model is $\emptyset$. But its completion

$$p \leftrightarrow p$$

is a tautology, and it has the same two stable models as (5.7): $\emptyset$ and $\{p\}$. Another example is given by the program

$$p \leftarrow q,$$
$$q \leftarrow p \wedge \neg r. \qquad (6.19)$$

Since r does not occur in the heads of these rules, (6.19) has the same stable models as the definite program

$$p \leftarrow q,$$
$$q \leftarrow p,$$
(6.20)

which means that its only stable model is Ø. But its completion

$$p \leftrightarrow q,$$
$$q \leftrightarrow p \wedge \neg r,$$
$$r \leftrightarrow \bot$$

has two stable models, Ø and $\{p, q\}$.

A condition that eliminates the cases when models of completion and stable models do not match is discussed in the next section.

6.4 Theorem on Completion

About a propositional program Π satisfying condition (α) and atomic formulas p, q we will say that p *depends* on q in Π if Π contains a rule $p \leftarrow F$ such that F contains an occurrence of q that is not in the scope of negation. In program (5.1), for example, p and q do not depend on any atoms; r depends on p but not on s; s depends on q.

The statement of the theorem below refers to the following additional condition on propositional programs:

(γ) it is possible to assign a nonnegative integer, called *the rank*, to every atomic formula occurring in the program, so that the rank of each atomic formula is greater than the ranks of the atomic formulas that it depends on.

For instance, program (5.1) satisfies not only conditions (α) and (β), but also condition (γ): we can assign rank 0 to p and q, and rank 1 to r and s. Condition (γ) is trivially satisfied for the rule $p \leftarrow \neg\neg p$ and for program (5.10) on page 80, because all occurrences of atoms in the bodies of all these rules are in the scope of negation.

On the other hand, condition (γ) does not hold for any program containing the rule $p \leftarrow p$: in application to such a program, this condition requires that the rank of p be greater than itself. Programs (6.19) and (6.20) do not satisfy condition (γ) either: the rank of p cannot be both greater than the rank of q, and less than it.

Another example when condition (γ) is not satisfied is given by the propositional image of the second rule in the recursive definition (2.8) of `ancestor/2`:

$$anc(v_1, v_3) \leftarrow anc(v_1, v_2) \wedge anc(v_2, v_3) \qquad (v_1, v_2, v_3 \in \mathbf{S} \cup \mathbf{Z}).$$

For a rule of this form with $v_1 = v_2 = v_3$, condition (γ) requires that the rank of $anc(v_1, v_1)$ be greater than itself.

Exercise 6.9 Determine whether program (4.2)–(4.5) on page 57 satisfies condition (γ).

Theorem on Completion *For any propositional program Π satisfying conditions (α) and (β), every stable model of Π is a model of the completion of Π. If Π satisfies also condition (γ) then the converse holds as well: every model of the completion of Π is a stable model of Π.*

Theorem on Completion can help us find the stable models of a propositional program satisfying conditions (α) and (β). We form a completion of such a program, and then find its models—either manually, as in the examples above, or by running a satisfiability solver. If the program satisfies condition (γ) then the result is the collection of stable models of the program. If not then some models of the completion may not be stable; they can be sifted out using the definition of a stable model in terms of reducts, as in Sect. 5.2.

Exercise 6.10 Use Theorem on Completion to find the stable models of

(a) program (5.10) on page 80,
(b) the program

$$p \leftarrow \neg q,$$
$$q \leftarrow \neg r,$$
$$r \leftarrow \neg p.$$

Exercise 6.11 Use Theorem on Completion to confirm your answer to Exercise 5.4 (page 75).

Theorem on Completion is not limited to finite programs. Consider, for instance, two infinite definite programs:

$$p_1 \leftarrow p_0,$$
$$p_2 \leftarrow p_1, \qquad\qquad\qquad (6.21)$$
$$\dots$$

and

$$p_0 \leftarrow p_1,$$
$$p_1 \leftarrow p_2, \qquad\qquad\qquad (6.22)$$
$$\dots\ .$$

Each of them has one stable model—the minimal model $\emptyset$. The former satisfies conditions (α)–(γ). (To verify (γ), assign rank n to p_n.) Its completion consists of the formulas

$$p_0 \leftrightarrow \bot,$$
$$p_1 \leftrightarrow p_0,$$
$$p_2 \leftrightarrow p_1,$$
$$\ldots,$$

and $\emptyset$ is the only model of the completion, in accordance with the theorem. Program (6.22), on the other hand, does not satisfy condition (γ). Indeed, in application to that program condition (γ) requires that the ranks of the atomic formulas $p_0, p_1, \ldots$ form a decreasing infinite sequence of nonnegative integers, which is impossible. The completion of this program

$$p_0 \leftrightarrow p_1,$$
$$p_1 \leftrightarrow p_2,$$
$$\ldots$$

has two models: $\emptyset$, which is stable, and $\{p_0, p_1, \ldots\}$, which is not.

In Sect. 5.5 we used Theorem on Facts to calculate the stable model of CLINGO program (5.11). The stable model of that program can be calculated also on the basis of Theorem on Completion. The completion of the propositional image (5.12) of the program is

$$p(a) \leftrightarrow \top,$$
$$p(v) \leftrightarrow \bot \qquad \text{for all } v \text{ other than } a,$$
$$q(a) \leftrightarrow \top,$$
$$q(v) \leftrightarrow \bot \qquad \text{for all } v \text{ other than } a,$$
$$r(v) \leftrightarrow p(v) \wedge \neg q(v) \qquad \text{for all } v.$$

The first four lines allow us to replace the last line by

$$r(a) \leftrightarrow \top \wedge \neg\top,$$
$$r(v) \leftrightarrow \bot \wedge \neg\bot \qquad \text{for all } v \text{ other than } a,$$

or, equivalently,

$$r(v) \leftrightarrow \bot \qquad \text{for all } v.$$

Consequently the only model of the completion is $\{p(a), q(a)\}$. Since (5.12) satisfies conditions (α)–(γ), it follows that $\{p(a), q(a)\}$ is the only stable model of program (5.11).

Exercise 6.12 Use Theorem on Completion to find all stable models of program (2.9), (2.10) on page 16.

6.5   Bibliographical and Historical Remarks

Equivalence relations between propositional formulas that are stronger than classical equivalence and do not treat, for instance, dropping a double negation as an
equivalent transformation have been studied in logic for a long time. This work
was initially related to the intuitionist philosophy of mathematics. The idea that
mathematics is the creation of the mind has led intuitionists to the view that the
law of excluded middle and "the principle that for every system the correctness of
a property follows from the impossibility of the impossibility of the property" may
be invalid in application to infinite systems [16].

The logical consequences of this view were clarified in 1930 by the invention
of intuitionistic propositional logic—a formal system that does not sanction the
law of excluded middle and other tautologies that intuitionists find objectionable
[66]. That paper included a theorem showing that the law of excluded middle is
not intuitionistically provable, so that intuitionistic logic is indeed weaker than
classical. The logic of here-and-there was introduced in the proof of that theorem as
a technical tool.

The fact that the logic of here-and-there is related to stable models was observed
in 1997 [101], and Theorem on Strong Equivalence was proved in 2001 [82].

Program completion was proposed as an explanation of the meaning of negation
as failure in 1978 [25], long before the invention of stable models, and generalized
in 1984 [87]. The definitions in these papers apply to rules with variables directly
and do not require that specific values be substituted for variables, as the version in
this book. In the style of the original definition, the completion of program (6.14)
would be written as

$$\forall X (q(X) \leftrightarrow \exists Y \, p(X, Y)).$$

The first result on the relationship between completion and stable models was
published in 1994 [35] and later extended to other classes of programs [32, 33, 64].
These papers define properties of programs similar to our condition (γ), and
programs with these properties are usually referred to as "tight." The definitions
of tightness in these papers are not expressed in terms of assigning ranks to
atomic formulas; they require instead that it should be impossible to find an infinite
sequence of atomic formulas such that every member of the sequence depends on
its successor. Tightness conditions of this kind are more general than condition (γ).
Consider, for instance, the infinite program

$$q \leftarrow p_0, \qquad p_1 \leftarrow p_0,$$
$$q \leftarrow p_1, \qquad p_2 \leftarrow p_1,$$
$$q \leftarrow p_2, \qquad p_3 \leftarrow p_2,$$
$$\cdots .$$

In this case, there is no infinite sequence of atomic formulas such that every member of the sequence depends on its successor. But finite sequences with this property that start with q can be arbitrarily long:

$$q, p_n, p_{n-1}, \ldots, p_1, p_0.$$

It follows that this program does not satisfy condition (γ). Programs like this will be covered if we modify condition (γ) by allowing ranks to be infinite ordinals $\omega, \omega + 1, \ldots$

If a program is not tight then its stable models can be described as the models of its completion that satisfy additional "loop formulas" [85]. This fact has been used in the design of answer set solvers [76, 85].

Chapter 7
More About the Language of CLINGO

The programming constructs described below significantly extend the expressive possibilities of the language used Chaps. 2 and 3. The first three sections are about *aggregates*—functions that apply to sets. Then we show how CLINGO can be used to solve combinatorial optimization problems and discuss CLINGO programs with symbolic functions and classical negation.

7.1 Counting

The aggregate #count calculates the number of elements of a set. For example, the expression

$$\#count\{X,Y \; : \; edge(X,Y)\}$$

represents the number of elements of the set edge/2. Expressions like this are used in the bodies of rules as one side of a comparison, with a term on the other side:

$$number\_of\_edges(N) \; :- \; N = \#count\{X,Y \; : \; edge(X,Y)\}.$$
(7.1)

The stable model of the program obtained by adding this rule to the definition (3.2) of a graph contains the atom number_of_edges(9): the graph has nine edges.

The part of an aggregate expression to the right of the colon may be a list of several atoms, negated atoms, and comparisons. For example, the expression

$$\#count\{X,Y,Z \; : \; edge(X,Y), \; edge(Y,Z)\}$$

denotes the number of paths of length 2, and the expression

© Springer Nature Switzerland AG 2019
V. Lifschitz, *Answer Set Programming*,
https://doi.org/10.1007/978-3-030-24658-7_7

$$\#count\{X,Y : edge(X,Y), X != a\}$$

denotes the number of edges with the tail different from a.

The part of an aggregate expression to the left of the colon may include not only variables, but also more complex terms. For example, if n is a placeholder for a positive integer then the expression

$$\#count\{X*Y : X = 2..n, Y = 2..n, X*Y <= n\}$$

calculates the number of composite numbers between 1 and n.

In rule (7.1), the variables X and Y are local: all their occurrences are between braces (see Sect. 2.6). An aggregate expression can contain also global variables. For instance, the outdegrees of vertices of a graph can be defined by the rule

```
outdegree(X,N) :- vertex(X), N = #count{Y : edge(X,Y)}.
```

In this rule, the variables X and N are global.

Aggregate expressions can be used in inequalities. For instance, the set of vertices of outdegree greater than 1 can be defined by the rule

```
branching_vertex(X) :- vertex(X),
             #count{Y : edge(X,Y)} > 1.
```

Note that a comparison cannot contain aggregate expressions on both sides. When we want to compare the values of two aggregate expressions, this can be accomplished by comparing each of them with the value of a variable. For instance, call a vertex *balanced* if its indegree equals its outdegree; the set of balanced vertices can be defined by the rule

```
balanced(X) :- vertex(X), #count{Y : edge(X,Y)} = N,
             #count{Y : edge(Y,X)} = N.
```

Exercise 7.1 The choice rule

$$\{in(1..n)\} = m.$$

(found, for example, in Line 10 of Listing 3.8, page 38) can be replaced by the combination of the rule

$$\{in(1..n)\}.$$

with a constraint. What constraint is that?

Listing 7.1 Number of classes (Exercise 7.2)

```
1   % Number of classes taught on each floor.
2
3   % input: number k of floors; set where/2 of all pairs (c,i)
4   %        such that class c is taught on the i-th floor.
5
6   _____
7   % achieved: howmany(I,N) iff the number of classes taught
8   %           on the I-th floor is N.
9
10  #show howmany/2.
```

Fig. 7.1 Solution to a
skyscraper puzzle

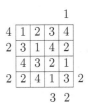

Exercise 7.2 We would like to write a CLINGO program that calculates the number of classes taught today on each floor of a classroom building. What rule would you place in Line 6 of Listing 7.1?

Exercise 7.3 Rule (1.1) defines a large country as a country inhabited by more people than the United Kingdom. How will you modify that rule if "large country" is understood as a country with a population that places it

1. among the top k countries on the given list?
2. in the top half of the countries on the given list?

We will see now how the #count aggregate is used in a CLINGO program that solves skyscraper puzzles. In such a puzzle, the goal is to fill an $n \times n$ grid with numbers from 1 to n. No number may be repeated in any row or column. The numbers represent the heights of skyscrapers, and they should be chosen according to clues—numbers placed around the perimeter of the grid. (See Fig. 7.1 for an example.) Each clue tells us how many buildings can be seen from that point, assuming that higher skyscrapers block the view of lower skyscrapers located behind them.

In Listing 7.2, the position of each clue is represented by the row and column where the clue is located. The clues to the left and above the grid are in row 0 and column 0, respectively; the clues to the right and below the grid are in row $n + 1$ and column $n + 1$. For example, the set clue/3 representing the puzzle in Fig. 7.1 is defined by the rule

```
clue(1,0,4;  2,0,2;  4,0,2;  0,4,1;  4,5,2;  5,3,3;  5,4,2).
```

Listing 7.2 Skyscrapers puzzle

```
1  % Skyscrapers puzzle.
2
3  % input: size n of the grid; set clue/3 of triples r,c,n
4  %        such that clue n is placed in row r, column c
5  %        around the perimeter of the grid.
6
7  % h(R,C,H) means that the height of the skyscraper in row R
8  % and column C is H.
9
10 {h(R,C,1..n)} = 1 :- R = 1..n, C = 1..n.
11 % achieved: every square of the grid is filled with a number
12 %           between 1 and n.
13
14 :- not h(R,_,H), R = 1..n, H = 1..n.
15 :- not h(_,C,H), C = 1..n, H = 1..n.
16 % achieved: every number between 1 and n occurs in every row
17 %           and every column.
18
19    blocked(R,C,0,C)   :- h(R,C,H), h(R1,C,H1), R1 < R, H1 > H.
20 blocked(R,C,n+1,C)   :- h(R,C,H), h(R1,C,H1), R1 > R, H1 > H.
21    blocked(R,C,R,0)   :- h(R,C,H), h(R,C1,H1), C1 < C, H1 > H.
22 blocked(R,C,R,n+1)   :- h(R,C,H), h(R,C1,H1), C1 > C, H1 > H.
23 % achieved: blocked(R,C,R0,C0) iff the skyscraper in row R,
24 %           column C is not visible from the observation
25 %           point in row R0, column C0.
26
27 :- clue(R0,C0,N), #count{R,C : blocked(R,C,R0,C0)} != n-N.
28 % achieved: clues match the numbers of visible skyscrapers.
29
30 #show h/3.
```

The constraint in Line 27 of the program says that the number of skyscrapers blocked from view cannot be different from $n - N$, where N is the value of the corresponding clue.

7.2 Summation

The aggregate #sum calculates the sum of a set of integers. For example, the set q/1 defined by the rule

$$q(N) :- N = \#sum\{X*X : p(X)\}.$$

is a singleton, and its only element is the sum of the squares of all integers in the set p/1. The program consisting of that rule and the rule

$$p(a; 1; 2).$$

has the stable model

$$\{p(a), p(1), p(2), q(5)\},$$

because $1^2 + 2^2 = 5$. Since the element a of p/1 is not an integer, it is disregarded in the process of adding squares.

If #sum is applied to an expression containing several terms to the left of the colon then the value of #sum can be described in terms of "weights." The *weight* of a tuple consisting of integers and symbolic constants is the first member of the tuple. What #sum calculates in application to a set of tuples is the sum of the weights of all its elements that have integer weights. For example, if the predicate size/2 is defined by rules (1.2) on page 3 then the expression

$$\#\text{sum}\{S,C\ :\ \text{size}(C,S)\,\}\tag{7.2}$$

represents the total population of the countries in Table 1.1.

There is subtle—but important—difference between aggregate expression (7.2) and the shorter expression

$$\#\text{sum}\{S\ :\ \text{size}(C,S)\,\}.\tag{7.3}$$

The former denotes the sum of the numbers s over all pairs (c, s) that belong to the set size/2. The latter denotes the sum of all numbers s such that for some c, (c, s) is an element of size/2. These sums may be different if the set includes two pairs with the same second member. For instance, if size/2 is defined by the rule

$$\text{size}(a,1;\ b,2;\ c,2).$$

then the value of (7.2) is 5, and the value of (7.3) is 3. Since the population sizes of all countries in Table 1.1 are different from each other, expression (7.3) has in that case the same value as (7.2).

Exercise 7.4 What is the stable model of the program

```
p(N)  :- N = #sum{X*X : X = -1..1}.
q(N)  :- N = #sum{X*X, X : X = -1..1}.
```

in your opinion?

Exercise 7.5 Simplify the aggregate expression $\#\text{sum}\{1,X\ :\ p(X)\,\}$.

Exercise 7.6 A *magic square* of size n is an $n \times n$ square grid filled with distinct integers in the range $1, \ldots, n^2$ so that the sum of numbers in each row, each column, and each of the two diagonals equals the same "magic constant." It is clear that the value of the magic constant is determined by the size of the square: it is

Listing 7.3 Magic squares (Exercise 7.6)

```
1  % Magic squares of size n
2
3  % input: positive integer n.
4
5  1 {filled(R,C,1..n*n)} 1 :- R = 1..n, C = 1..n.
6  % achieved: every square of the grid is filled with a number
7  %            between 1 and n^2.
8
9  :- not filled(_,_,X), X = 1..n*n.
10 % achieved: every number between 1 and n^2 is included.
11
12 #const magic=(n**3+n)/2.
13
14 _____
15 % achieved: every row sums up to magic.
16
17 _____
18 % achieved: every column sums up to magic.
19
20 _____
21 _____
22 % achieved: both diagonals sum up to magic.
```

$(1 + 2 + \cdots + n^2)/n$, which equals $(n + n^3)/2$. We would like to write a CLINGO program that generates all magic squares of a given size. The rules in Lines 5 and 9 of Listing 7.3 are the same as in Listing 3.16 (page 43). What rules would you place in Lines 14, 17, 20, 21?

The next example of using the #sum aggregate is motivated by the problem of determining the winner when voters rank several options or candidates in order of preference. One possibility is to calculate the number of points assigned to each candidate by each voter, as follows: the candidate ranked last gets zero points; next to last gets one point, and so on. Once all votes have been counted, the candidate with the most points is the winner. There are several winners in case of a tie.

For example, assume that Andy, Bob and Charlie run for the same office; the ranking $C > B > A$ is chosen by 400 voters, $B > C > A$ by 200 voters, and $A > B > C$ by 300 voters. Then

Andy gets $300 \times 2 = 600$ points,
Bob gets $400 \times 1 + 200 \times 2 + 300 \times 1 = 1100$ points,
Charlie gets $400 \times 2 + 200 \times 1 = 1000$ points;

Bob is the winner.

The program in Listing 7.4 calculates the winner in accordance with this procedure. The example above can be represented by the following input:

Listing 7.4 Choosing winners in an election with multiple candidates

```
1  % Choose the winner according to the number of points earned
2  % by each candidate.
3
4  % input: the number m of candidates 1,...,m; the set
5  %        votecount/2 of pairs (R,N) such that ranking R
6  %        was selected by N voters; the set p/3 of triples
7  %        (R,Pos,C) such that Pos is the position of
8  %        candidate C in ranking R.
9
10 posScore(R,C,X*N) :- p(R,Pos,C), X = m-Pos, votecount(R,N).
11 % achieved: posScore(R,C,S) iff the voters who chose
12 %           ranking R contributed S points to candidate C.
13
14 score(C,N) :- C = 1..m, N = #sum{S,R : posScore(R,C,S)}.
15 % achieved: score(C,N) iff candidate C earned N points.
16
17 loser(C) :- score(C,N), score(C1,N1), N1 > N.
18 % achieved: loser(C) iff candidate C earned fewer points
19 %           than another candidate.
20
21 winner(C) :- C = 1..m, not loser(C).
22 % achieved: winner(C) iff C is a winner.
23
24 #show winner/1.
```

```
#const m=3.
votecount(1,400; 2,200; 3,300).
p(1,1,3; 1,2,2; 1,3,1;
  2,1,2; 2,2,3; 2,3,1;
  3,1,1; 3,2,2; 3,3,3).
```

Note that in the aggregate expression

$$\#sum\{S,R \; : \; posScore(R,C,S)\}$$

(Line 14 of the program) the number S of points to the left of the colon is followed by the number R of the ranking that contributed these points. This is essential when a candidate receives the same number of points from different rankings; without R appended to S in this expression, the number of points earned by such a candidate would be calculated incorrectly. This would happen, in fact, in the example above, because Bob gets 400 points from the voters who chose the ranking $C > B > A$, and the same number of points from the voters who chose $B > C > A$. If we replace S,R in Line 14 by S then CLINGO will tell us, incorrectly, that Charlie is the winner.

Exercise 7.7 Write a program that takes the same input as the program in Listing 7.4 and calculates the winner in accordance with the following procedure. The candidates are compared pairwise. In case one candidate is preferred by more voters he receives one point, the other candidate receives zero points. In case of a tie, each receives 0.5 points. The candidate's score is the sum of all points he receives. In the example above, Andy is rated higher than Bob by 300 voters, and Bob is rated higher than Andy by 600 voters; that gives Bob one point. Bob is rated higher than Charlie by 500 voters, and Charlie is rated higher than Bob by 400 voters; that gives Bob one more point. As a result, Bob's final score is 2. Andy's score is 0, and Charlie's score is 1, so that Bob is declared the winner.

7.3   Maximum and Minimum

The aggregates #max and #min represent the largest and the smallest elements of a set. For instance, the expression

$$\#max\{X : p(X)\}$$

calculates the largest element of the set p/1, and the expression

$$\#min\ |X-Y|: p(X), q(Y)\}$$

calculates the distance between sets p/1 and q/1 of integers (that is, the smallest among the distances from elements of p/1 to elements of q/1).

The total order chosen by the designers of CLINGO for evaluating comparisons (Sect. 2.1) is defined not only on numbers and symbolic constants, but also on two additional ground terms: the symbols #inf and #sup. The former is the least element of that total order, and the latter is its greatest element:

```
#inf   ...   -7  -6  -5  ...   5  6  7  ...  abc  ...  #sup
```

In application to the empty set, #max returns #inf, and #min returns #sup. This is similar to the convention mentioned in Sect. 4.2: the sum of the empty set of numbers is 0, and the product is 1.

Exercise 7.8 Adding the constraint

```
:- not p(_).
```

to a CLINGO program eliminates the stable models in which the set p/1 is empty (Sect. 2.8). Find constraints with the same property that use, instead of an anonymous variable, (a) the aggregate #count, (b) the aggregate #max, (c) the aggregate #min.

The definition of `winner/1` in terms of the auxiliary predicate `loser/1` in Lines 17–21 of Listing 7.4 can be replaced by a more concise definition using the aggregate #max:

```
winner(C)  :- score(C,N), N = #max{N1 : score(C1,N1)}.
```

The encoding of Hamiltonian cycles in Listing 3.14 (page 41) expects an input that specifies, in addition to the predicates `vertex/1` and `edge/2`, one of the vertices `v0` of the graph. The symbol `v0` is used in the first rule

```
reachable(X)  :- in(v0,X).
```

of the recursive definition of `reachable/1`. The need to specify `v0` will be eliminated if we rewrite that rule as

```
reachable(X)  :- in(V0,X), V0 = #max{V : vertex(V)}.
```

The aggregate #min would work here as well, of course.

Exercise 7.9 The program from Exercise 7.2 (page 110) determines the number of classes taught on each floor of a building using two pieces of information: the number k of floors and the set of pairs (c, i) such that class c is taught on floor i. Under the assumption that at least one class is taught on the top floor, there is no need to include the value of k in the input. Under this assumption, what rule will you place in Line 6 of Listing 7.1 if the value of k is not given?

The run-time of CLINGO on the encoding of Schur numbers in Listing 3.6 (page 34) can be improved by including a symmetry breaking constraint that forces the first sum-free subset to include 1, the second to include the smallest number that does not belong to the first, and so on. This can be expressed using the #min aggregate:

```
:- K = 1..r-1, M = #min{I : in(I,K)},
             M > #min{I : in(I,K+1)}.
```

7.4 Optimization

When a logic program has several stable models, we may be interested in finding its stable model that is good, or even the best possible, according to some measure of quality. A measure of quality can be specified by an aggregate expression. For instance, the expression

$$\#sum\{X : p(X)\} \tag{7.4}$$

Listing 7.5 Knapsack problem

```
1  % Knapsack problem.
2
3  % input: set weight/2 of pairs (i,w) such that w is the weight
4  %          of item i; set value/2 of pairs (i,v) such that v is
5  %          the value of item i; limit maxweight on the total
6  %          weight.
7
8  {in(I)} :- weight(I,W).
9  % achieved: in/1 is a subset of the set of items.
10
11 :- #sum{W,I : in(I), weight(I,W)} > maxweight.
12 % achieved: the total weight of items in this subset doesn't
13 %              exceed maxweight.
14
15 % optimize the selection.
16 #maximize{V,I : in(I), value(I,V)}.
17
18 #show in/1.
```

measures the quality of a stable model by the sum of the integers in the set p/1; the model in which this sum is the largest or the smallest would be considered the best.

The directives #maximize and #minimize instruct CLINGO to improve the first stable model that it generated using a #sum aggregate expression as the measure of quality, and to keep looking for better and better stable models until the best model is found. For example, the directive

$$\#maximize\{X : p(X)\}$$

will cause CLINGO to generate stable models in which the values of aggregate expression (7.4) are larger and larger. These directives allow us to apply CLINGO to combinatorial optimization problems, where the goal is to find the best among several alternatives.

Consider, for instance, the knapsack problem, where we are given a set of items, each with a weight and a value, and the goal is to determine which items to include in a collection so that the total weight does not exceed a given limit and the total value is as large as possible. This problem is encoded in Listing 7.5. Given this program and the input

```
weight(a,12; b,1; c,4; d,2; e,1).
value(a,4; b,2; c, 10; d,2; e,1).
#const maxweight=15.
```

CLINGO will produce an output like this:

```
Answer: 1

Optimization: 0
Answer: 2
in(b)
Optimization: -2
Answer: 3
in(b) in(e)
Optimization: -3
Answer: 4
in(b) in(d)
Optimization: -4


. . . . . . . . .


Answer: 11
in(b) in(c) in(d) in(e)
Optimization: -15
OPTIMUM FOUND
```

In every answer, the number after the word Optimization shows the total weight of the items in the set in/1. (The minus sign is prepended by CLINGO whenever the #maximize directive is used, rather than #minimize.)

Exercise 7.10 We would like to restrict not only the total weight of the selected items, but also their combined volume. The set volume/2 consists of the pairs (i, vol) such that vol is the volume of item i; maxvolume is the upper bound on the combined volume. How would you modify the program in Listing 7.5 to encode this enhancement of the basic knapsack problem?

Exercise 7.11 In the "unbounded" version of the knapsack problem, an unlimited number of copies of each kind of item is available. What rules would you place in Lines 10 and 15 of Listing 7.6, and what directive in Line 20, to solve this version of the problem?

The program in Listing 7.7 is a modification of the coloring program from Exercise 3.13 (page 38) that colors a graph using the smallest possible number of colors, and thus calculates its chromatic number. Integers between 1 and the number N of vertices of the graph are used as colors. (It is clear that the chromatic number never exceeds N.) The directive in Line 19 exploits the fact that the aggregate expression

$$\#sum\{1, C \; : \; color(X, C)\}$$

has the same meaning as

$$\#count\{C \; : \; color(X, C)\}$$

Listing 7.6 Unbounded knapsack problem (Exercise 7.11)

```
1  % Unbounded knapsack problem.
2
3  % input: set weight/3 of pairs (i,w) such that w is the weight
4  %          of item 1; set value/3 of pairs (i,v) such that v is
5  %          the value of item i; limit maxweight on the total
6  %          weight.
7
8  % in(I,N) means that N copies of item I are selected.
9
10 _____
11 % achieved: in/2 is a set of pairs(i,n) such that i is an item
12 %            and n is a nonnegative integer such that the
13 %            weight of n copies of i doesn't exceed maxweight.
14
15 _____
16 % achieved: the total weight of selected items doesn't exceed
17 %            maxweight.
18
19 % optimize the selection.
20 _____
21
22 #show in/2.
```

Listing 7.7 Graph coloring using the minimal number of colors

```
1  % Color the vertices of a graph using the minimal number
2  % of colors.
3
4  % input: set vertex/1 of vertices of a graph G; set edge/2
5  %          of edges of G.
6
7  % color(X,C) means that the color of vertex X is C.
8
9  {color(X,1..N)} = 1 :- vertex(X),
10                        N = #count{Y : vertex(Y)}.
11 % achieved: for every vertex X there is a unique C from
12 %            {1,...,N} such that color(X,C), where N is
13 %            the number of vertices of G.
14
15 :- edge(X,Y), color(X,C), color(Y,C).
16 % achieved: no two adjacent vertices share the same color.
17
18 % minimize the numbers of colors.
19 #minimize{1,C : color(X,C)}.
20
21 #show color/2.
```

Listing 7.8 Optimization version of set packing (Exercise 7.12)

```
1  % Find the largest possible number of pairwise disjoint
2  % members of a given list of finite sets.
3
4  % input: for a list S_1,...,S_n of sets, its length n and
5  %          the set s/2 of pairs X,I such that X is in S_I.
6
7  % in(I) means that set S_I is included in the solution.
8
9  {in(1..n)}.
10 % achieved: in/1 is a set of members of the list.
11
12 I = J :- in(I), in(J), s(X,I), s(X,J).
13 % achieved: the chosen sets are pairwise disjoint.
14
15 % maximize the number of chosen sets
16 _____
17
18 #show in/1.
```

(see Exercise 7.5). If we replace 1, C in that line by C then CLINGO will minimize the *sum* of the numbers used as colors. As a result, the colors that we will see in an optimal solution will be small integers, between 1 and the chromatic number of the graph. This modification will also cause CLINGO to terminate faster, because of its symmetry breaking effect.

Exercise 7.12 We would like to solve the optimization version of the set packing problem (Sect. 3.5), which calls for finding the largest possible number of pairwise disjoint members of a given list of finite sets. What directive would you place in Line 16 of Listing 7.8?

Exercise 7.13 Recall that a clique in a graph is a subset of its vertices such that every two distinct vertices in it are adjacent (Sect. 3.6). We would like to write a CLINGO program that finds the largest clique in a given graph. What rule would you place in Line 6 of Listing 7.9, and what directive in Line 13, to achieve this goal?

Exercise 7.14 Research papers submitted to a technical conference are reviewed by the conference program committee. Every paper is read and discussed by a group of committee members chosen by the chair of the committee, and this group decides if the paper can be accepted for presentation. To help the chair find a good match between papers and referees, every committee member submits a bid that classifies all papers that need to be reviewed into three categories: "yes" (I want to review this paper), "maybe" (I do not mind reviewing it), and "no" (do not assign it to me). We would like to write a program for CLINGO that automates this part of the work of the chair. Using a list of bids, it should assign each submitted paper for review to a specific number k of committee members so that

Listing 7.9 The largest clique (Exercise 7.13)

```
 1  % Find the largest clique.
 2
 3  % input: set vertex/1 of vertices of a graph G;
 4  %         set edge/2 of edges of G.
 5
 6  _____
 7  % achieved: in/1 is a set of vertices of G.
 8
 9  X = Y :- in(X), in(Y), not edge(X,Y), not edge(Y,X).
10  % achieved: in/1 is a clique.
11
12  % maximize the size of the clique.
13  _____
14
15  #show in/1.
```

- the workloads of committee members are approximately equal—do not differ by more than 1;
- no committee member is asked to review a submission that he placed in the "no" group;
- the total number of cases when a submission is assigned to a reviewer who placed it in the "yes" group is as large as possible.

What rules would you place in Lines 7, 11, 17, 22, and 26 of Listing 7.10, and what directive in Line 31, to achieve this goal?

7.5 Symbolic Functions

In the programs that we have seen so far, all terms are formed from constants and variables using arithmetic operations. The syntax of CLINGO allows us to form terms also in another way—using a symbolic constant as the name of a function. A symbolic constant followed by a list of terms (separated by commas) in parentheses is a term. For instance, the expressions f(X,Y) and f(g(a),10) are terms that use f as a function of two variables and g as a function of one variable. The expression p(f(X,Y),f(g(a),10)) is an atom, and f(X,Y) != Z is a comparison.

Terms containing a symbolic function are similar to records in imperative programming languages.

In this more general setting, an extra clause needs to be added to the recursive definition of the set of values of a ground term given in Sect. 4.6:

5. If t is $f(t_1, \ldots, t_k)$ then the values of t are terms of the form $f(v_1, \ldots, v_k)$, where $v_1, \ldots, v_k$ are values of $t_1, \ldots, t_k$ respectively.

Listing 7.10 Assigning papers to referees (Exercise 7.14)

```
1   % Assigning papers to referees.
2
3   % input: set bid/3 of triples (r,p,b) such that b is bid
4   %          ("yes", "no", or "maybe") submitted by referee r
5   %          for paper p; positive integer k.
6
7   _____
8   % achieved: referee/1 is the set of referees who submitted
9   %          bids.
10
11  _____
12  % achieved: paper/1 is the set of papers for which bids are
13  %          submitted.
14
15  % review(R,P) means that paper P is assigned to referee R.
16
17  _____
18  % achieved: for every paper P there are exactly k referees R
19  %          such that review(R,P); the bids submitted by
20  %          these referees for P are different from "no".
21
22  _____
23  % achieved: workload(R,N) iff N is the number of papers
24  %          assigned for review to referee R.
25
26  _____
27  % achieved: the difference between the workloads of
28  %          referees is at most 1.
29
30  % maximize the number of "yes" cases.
31  _____
32
33  #show review/2.
```

For instance, the only value of f(a,g(2+2)) is f(a,g(4)).

Exercise 7.15 Find all values of the term f(1..2,g(1..2)).

Exercise 7.16 What stable models do you think will be produced by CLINGO for the following programs?

(a)   p :- f(1,2) = 7.
(b)   p(f(1..2,g(1..2))).
       q(X):- p(f(_,X)).

Symbolic functions can be used, for instance, to describe points in a coordinate plane. The graph shown in Fig. 7.2 can be represented by the rules

Fig. 7.2 Graph with 16
vertices and 24 edges

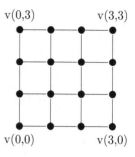

v(0,3)   v(3,3)

v(0,0)   v(3,0)

```
vertex(v(0..3,0..3)).
edge(v(R,C),v(R,C+1))  :- R = 0..3, C = 0..2.
edge(v(R,C),v(R+1,C))  :- R = 0..2, C = 0..3.
```

If we give these rules as input to the program in Listing 7.7 then CLINGO will
determine that the chromatic number of the graph is 2.

We will see other programs that use symbolic functions in Chap. 8.

7.6 Classical Negation

Recall that an atom is a symbolic constant that may be followed by a list of
arguments in parentheses (Sect. 2.1). A *negated atom* is an atom preceded by the
minus sign. When the minus sign is used to form a negated atom, it is called *classical*
(or *strong*) *negation*. About an atom and its classical negation we say that they are
complementary to each other. For example, the atom p(a) and the negated atom
-p(a) form a complementary pair.

Syntactically, a negated atom can be used in a CLINGO program wherever an
atom is allowed. Like an atom without classical negation, it can be preceded by one
or two negation as failure symbols. When CLINGO generates stable models, it treats
each classical negation as if it were an extra character at the beginning of a predicate
symbol, except that it does not display stable models that contain a complementary
pair. For example, CLINGO's answer to the program

```
p(1..2).
-p(3..4).
```

is

$$p(1) \ p(2) \ -p(3) \ -p(4)$$

but the program

```
p(1..2).
-p(2..3).
```

has no stable models. In response to the program

Listing 7.11 Coprime numbers encoded using classical negation

```
1  % Numbers from 1 to n that are coprime with k.
2
3  % input: positive integer n; integer k
4
5  -coprime(N)  :- N=1..n, I=2..N, N\I=0, k\I=0.
6  % achieved: -coprime/1 is the set of numbers from {1,...,n}
7  %              that are not coprime with k.
8
9  coprime(N)  :- N=1..n, not -coprime(N).
10 % achieved: coprime/1 is the set of numbers from {1,...,n}
11 %              that are coprime with k.
12
13 #show coprime/1.
```

```
{p(1..2)}.
-p(2..3).
```

CLINGO displays two answers,

$$-p(2)\ \ -p(3)$$

and

$$-p(2)\ \ -p(3)\ \ p(1)$$

—including p(2) is not an option, because it is complementary to -p(2).

Exercise 7.17 What stable models do you think will be produced by CLINGO for the following programs?

(a)   {p}.
      q :- not p.
      r :- -p.
(b)   {p}.
      q.
      -q :- not p.

If an encoding uses a pair of propositions with opposite meanings then it is convenient to denote one of them by a negated atom. For example, the program from Exercise 2.18 (page 17) uses the symbol coprime/1 for the set of numbers between 1 and n that are coprime with k, and the symbol noncoprime/1 for the set of numbers between 1 and n that do not have this property. Listing 7.11 shows the modification of that program in which noncoprime/1 is replaced by -coprime/1. Listing 7.12 shows the modification of the program from Exercise 2.19 in which more_than_three/1 is replaced by -three/1.

Listing 7.12 Integers requiring four squares encoded using classical negation

```
 1  % Numbers from 1 to n that cannot be represented as the sum
 2  % of 3 complete squares.
 3
 4  % input: positive integer n.
 5
 6  three(N) :- N=1..n, I=0..n, J=0..n, K=0..n, N=I**2+J**2+K**2.
 7  % achieved: three/1 is the set of numbers from {1,...,n} that
 8  %             can be represented as the sum of 3 squares.
 9
10  -three(N) :- N=1..n, not three(N).
11  % achieved: -three/1 is the set of numbers from {1,...,n} that
12  %             can't be represented as the sum of 3 squares.
13
14  #show -three/1.
```

In the last example, the rule in Line 10 expresses that a number between 1 and n cannot be represented as the sum of three squares if there is no evidence that it can. In other words, this rule represents the *closed world assumption* for the property `three/1` in the domain $\{1, \ldots, n\}$. The general form of closed world assumption rules is

$$-p(X) :- \cdots , not \ p(X).$$

where the part of the body denoted by dots describes the domain. The rule in Line 9 of Listing 7.11 expresses the opposite assumption about the property `coprime/1`: a number between 1 and n is coprime with k if there is no evidence that it is not.

Classical negation is useful for distinguishing between what is known to be false and what is unknown. For example, the facts

```
candidate(a; b; c; d; e).
elected(a; b).
-elected(c; d).
```

describe the status of five candidates in an election: a and b have won, c and d have lost, and the status of e is still undecided.

7.7   Bibliographical and Historical Remarks

The `#count` and `#sum` aggregates are inherited by CLINGO from two older answer set solvers, SMODELS [99] and DLV [75]. Propositional images of programs with aggregates [44] are syntactically more general than propositional rules in the sense of Sect. 4.1—they may contain implications in the body of an implication, as in the formula $p \leftarrow (q \leftarrow r)$. The definition of a stable model was extended to arbitrary propositional formulas in 2005 [37], and it has a simple characterization in terms of equilibrium logic [101].

Other definitions of stable models for programs with aggregates proposed in the literature [34, 55, 104, 113] are not equivalent to the semantics adopted by the designers of CLINGO, but differences can be seen mostly in artificially constructed counterexamples [63].

#maximize and #minimize directives appeared originally in SMODELS. In DLV, optimization is achieved using "weak constraints"; that mechanism is available in the language of CLINGO as well.

The approach to computing winners in an election presented in Sect. 7.2 is known as the *Borda rule*, and the process described in Exercise 7.7 is the *Copeland rule*. Many other rules of this kind have been proposed. The *k-approval rule*, for instance, where k is a positive integer, is similar to the Borda rule except that it assigns one point to each candidate who is ranked among the first k. (The case of $k = 1$ is called the *plurality rule*). According to the *veto rule*, the winner is the candidate who is ranked last by the smallest number of voters. The DEMOCRATIX system [20] encodes a large number of voting rules in the language of CLINGO, and it is used as a computational tool by researchers in the area of voting theory. DEMOCRATIX is available as a web application, along with its source code and the encodings of the voting rules, at http://democratix.dbai.tuwien.ac.at/.

Symbolic functions are inherited by answer set solvers from Prolog. They were covered by the original definition of a stable model [51].

Classical negation was added to the syntax of logic programs in 1990 [52, 102]. With this feature included in the language, the correspondence between rules and defaults mentioned in Sect. 5.9 is applicable to an arbitrary default (5.24) such that each of the formulas F_i, G_j, H in it is a literal (that is, an atom possibly prefixed by $\neg$). For example, the default

$$\frac{p_1, \neg p_2 \; : \; \mathsf{M} q_1, \mathsf{M} \neg q_2}{\neg r}$$

corresponds to the rule

```
-r :- p1, -p2, not -q1, not q2.
```

Informally, the meaning of logic programs with two kinds of negation can be described by three principles: satisfy the rules of the program; do not believe in contradictions; believe in nothing you are not forced to believe [50]. The first and the last of these principles correspond to clauses (i) and (ii) of the characterization of stable models on page 76; not believing in contradictions corresponds to eliminating the stable models containing complementary pairs.

The term "closed world assumption" was originally introduced in the context of deductive databases [106].

Chapter 8
Dynamic Systems

Answer set programming has important applications to the study of *dynamic systems*—systems whose states can be changed by performing actions. It can be used, for instance, to predict and to plan. In a prediction problem, the task is to determine how the current state of a dynamic system will change after executing a given sequence of actions. In a planning problem, the task is to find a sequence of actions that leads a dynamic system from a given initial state to a goal state.

In this chapter we describe the methodology of representing dynamic systems by logic programs and give examples of the use of CLINGO for prediction and planning.

8.1 Example: The Blocks World

The *blocks world* is the dynamic system that consists of several blocks stacked one on top of another, forming towers. Each tower is based on the table. If, for example, the blocks are a and b then the blocks world can be in 3 states, shown in Fig. 8.1. If the blocks are a, b, and c, then the blocks world can be in 13 states, shown in Fig. 8.2. The actions available in the blocks world are $move(x, y)$—"move x onto y"—where x is a block and y is either a block other than x or *table*. Such an action can be executed only if there are no blocks on top of x. (We imagine that blocks are moved by a robot's arm, which grasps them from above.) For example, the only actions executable in state S_7 (Fig. 8.2) are

$$move(a, c), \ move(a, table), \ move(c, a);$$

block b cannot be moved. Action $move(c, b)$ is not executable in that state because there is another block on top of b. Action $move(c, table)$ is not executable because c is already on the table.

© Springer Nature Switzerland AG 2019
V. Lifschitz, *Answer Set Programming*,
https://doi.org/10.1007/978-3-030-24658-7_8

Fig. 8.1 States of the blocks world with 2 blocks

```
a        b
b        a        a b
---      ---      -----

S₁       S₂       S₃
```

Here are examples of prediction and planning problems in the blocks world with the blocks a, b, c.

1. Assume that the blocks world is initially in state S_7. What is going to be the effect of executing the action $move(a, c)$ and then $move(b, a)$? The answer to this prediction question is that the blocks world will be in state S_2.
2. For the same initial state, what about executing the action $move(a, c)$ and then $move(b, c)$? Answer: this sequence of actions is not executable.
3. For the same initial state, if we would like b to be on top of c, what sequence of actions would accomplish this? One possible plan is

$$move(a, table); \ move(b, c).$$

To represent a prediction problem or a planning problem in the blocks world as a CLINGO program, we need to specify, among other things, the set of available blocks, for instance:

$$block(a; \ b; \ c). \tag{8.1}$$

Exercise 8.1 (a) In the initial state of the blocks world with n blocks, all blocks are on the table. What is the number of actions that can be performed in this state? (b) In the initial state of the blocks world, blocks form n towers, and every tower contains more than one block. What is the number of actions that can be performed? (c) Blocks are arranged in n towers, and m out of them contain more than one block. What is the number of actions that can be performed?

```
a       b       a       c       b       c
b       a       c       a       c       b
c       c       b       b       a       a
---     ---     ---     ---     ---     ---

S₁      S₂      S₃      S₄      S₅      S₆


a       b       a       c       b       c
b c     a c     c b     a b     c a     b a     a b c
-----   -----   -----   -----   -----   -----   -------

S₇      S₈      S₉      S₁₀     S₁₁     S₁₂     S₁₃
```

Fig. 8.2 States of the blocks world with 3 blocks

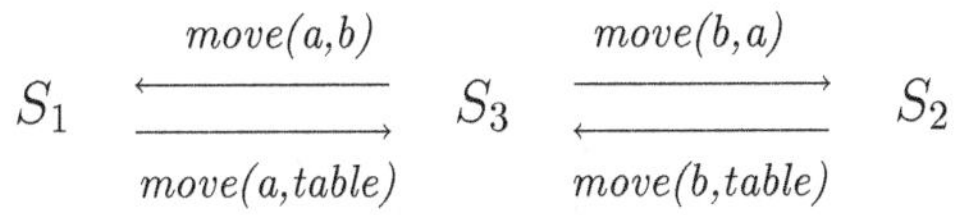

Fig. 8.3 Transition diagram
of the blocks world with 2
blocks

$$S_1 \xleftarrow{\;move(a,b)\;} S_3 \xrightarrow{\;move(b,a)\;} S_2$$
$$S_1 \xrightarrow{\;move(a,table)\;} \qquad S_2 \xleftarrow{\;move(b,table)\;}$$

Exercise 8.2 Give an example of a planning problem in the blocks world with 3 blocks that cannot be solved in fewer than 4 steps.

8.2 Transition Diagrams

A dynamic system can be graphically represented by the directed graph called its *transition diagram*. The vertices of this graph are the states of the system, and its edges are labeled by actions. The tail of an edge is the state in which the action started, and the head is the resulting state.

Figure 8.3 shows the transition diagram of the blocks world with 2 blocks. The transition diagram of the blocks world with blocks a, b, c has 3 edges starting at S_7:

$$\begin{array}{ll}
\text{edge labeled } move(a, c) \text{ leading to } S_9, & \\
\text{edge labeled } move(a, table) \text{ leading to } S_{13}, & (8.2) \\
\text{edge labeled } move(c, a) \text{ leading to } S_4. &
\end{array}$$

Exercise 8.3 In the transition diagram of the blocks world with 3 blocks, (a) what is the total number of edges? (b) how many of them lead to S_7? (c) how many of them are labeled $move(a, table)$?

A dynamic system is *deterministic* if, for every state S of the system and every action A, its transition diagram contains at most one edge that starts at S and is labeled A. The discussion in this chapter is limited to deterministic systems.

A prediction problem can be visualized as the problem of finding the end point of the path in the transition diagram that starts at the given vertex and consists of edges labeled by the given actions. For instance, the answer to question (i) from Sect. 8.1 tells us that the path beginning at vertex S_7 with the edges labeled $move(a, c)$ and $move(b, a)$ leads to vertex S_2. The answer to question (ii) tells us that no path starting at S_7 consists of edges labeled $move(a, c)$, $move(b, c)$.

A planning problem can be thought of as the problem of finding a path in the transition diagram that leads from the given initial state to the given set of goal states. For instance, question (iii) from Sect. 8.1 calls for finding a path from S_7 to any of the vertices S_1, S_5, S_{11}.

Exercise 8.4 (Turkey Shoot) Consider the dynamic system consisting of a gun, which can be loaded or unloaded, and a turkey, which can be alive or dead. This system can be in 4 states:

(loaded, alive), *(loaded, dead)*, *(unloaded, alive)*, *(unloaded, dead)*.

There are 2 actions: *load*, which can be executed whenever the gun is unloaded, and *shoot*, which can be executed whenever the gun is loaded. After shooting, the turkey is dead, and the gun is unloaded. Draw the transition diagram for this dynamic system.

Exercise 8.5 Consider the modification of the turkey shoot domain in which the action *shoot* is considered executable even when the gun is not loaded, although in that case shooting does not kill the turkey. How will this modification affect the transition diagram?

Exercise 8.6 (3-Way Bulbs) Consider the dynamic system consisting of several 3-way bulbs controlled by pull-chain switches. A switch can be in 4 positions: off (0), low (1), medium (2), and high (3). The system can be in 4^n states, represented by lists of numbers of length n, where n is the number of bulbs. The actions are *pull(i)*, "pull the chain controlling bulb i." (a) Draw the transition diagram describing this system for $n = 1$. (b) What is the total number of edges in the transition diagram for an arbitrary n? (c) Describe the edges starting at the vertex (0,0,3).

Exercise 8.7 (Crossing the River) You are on a river bank, with a boat and several items that you can take with you to the other bank. The boat, and each of the items, can be in one of two locations—on the left bank or on the right bank. These locations determine the state of the system. The items are bulky, so that the boat cannot carry more than one at a time. The available actions are *cross(x)*, where x is one of the items (cross the river taking x with you) or the symbol *empty*. (a) Assume that in state S the boat and all n items are on the left bank. What is the length of the shortest path in the transition diagram that leads from S to the state in which the boat and all items are on the right bank? (b) How many paths of length 2 in the transition diagram start at vertex S?

8.3   Time

To describe sequentially executed actions by a set of atoms, we need to represent time. Time instants will be denoted by integers between 0 and a nonnegative integer h ("horizon"), and the execution of an action will be assumed to take one unit of time. For example, we will think of scenario (i) from Sect. 8.1 as executing the action *move(a, c)* between times 0 and 1, and executing *move(b, a)* between times 1 and 2.

In a CLINGO program, this scenario can be represented by the directive

$$\#const\ h=2. \tag{8.3}$$

and the facts

$$\texttt{occurs (move (a,c) ,0) .} \qquad\qquad (8.4)$$

and

$$\texttt{occurs (move (b,a) ,1) .} \qquad\qquad (8.5)$$

The predicate *occurs* serves for specifying the time when the execution of an action begins. Note that the symbol move is used here as a symbolic function (see Sect. 7.5).

States of a dynamic system can be described in terms of parameters called *fluents*. In the case of the blocks world, locations of blocks can be used as fluents. For instance, state S_7 can be characterized by saying that the location of a is (the top of) b, the location of b is the table, and the location of c is the table also; symbolically,

$$loc(a, b), \ loc(b, table), \ loc(c, table).$$

The use of fluents to describe the state of a dynamic system is similar to the use of coordinates to describe the position of an object.

To specify the value of a fluent at a given time instant, we use the predicate *holds*. The atom holds $(\texttt{C}, \texttt{T})$ expresses that condition C holds at time T. For instance, the assumption that the blocks world with 3 blocks is in state S_7 at time 0 can be expressed by the facts

$$
\begin{aligned}
&\texttt{holds (loc (a,b) ,0) .}\\
&\texttt{holds (loc (b,table) ,0) .} \qquad\qquad (8.6)\\
&\texttt{holds (loc (c,table) ,0) .}
\end{aligned}
$$

Syntactically, the symbol loc, like move, is a symbolic function.

Exercise 8.8 States of the turkey shoot domain (Exercise 8.4) can be described by two fluents, *state_of_gun* with the values *loaded* and *unloaded*, and *state_of_turkey*, with the values *alive* and *dead*. For instance, the condition "the gun is loaded" can be represented by the term *state_of_gun*(*loaded*). Consider the following scenario: the turkey is initially alive, and the gun is unloaded; then the action *load* is executed, followed by *shoot*. How would you describe it by a directive and a set of atoms?

Exercise 8.9 States of the 3-way bulb domain (Exercise 8.6) with n bulbs can be described by n fluents with the values $0, \ldots, 3$. For instance, the condition "bulb I is off" can be represented by the term *brightness*(*bulb*(I), 0). Consider the following scenario: the system consisting of 3 bulbs is initially in the state (0,0,3), and then the action *pull*(3) is executed. How would you describe it by a directive and a set of atoms?

Exercise 8.10 States of the crossing the river domain (Exercise 8.7) can be described by the locations of the boat and of all the items. The possible values of these fluents are *left* and *right*. Consider the following scenario: there are two items, a and b; initially they are on the left bank, and the boat is on the right bank; you cross the river to bring both items to the right bank—first a and then b. How would you describe it by a directive and a set of atoms?

The requirement that at each time instant, each block must have a unique location can be expressed by the constraint

$$
\begin{aligned}
&\texttt{:- \#count\{L : holds(loc(B,L),T)\} != 1, block(B),}\\
&\texttt{T = 0..h.} \tag{8.7}
\end{aligned}
$$

Constraints requiring the existence and uniqueness of value of every fluent at every time instant, as in this example, will be included in all our encodings of dynamic domains.

Exercise 8.11 Write the existence and uniqueness of value constraints for the following domains:

(a) the turkey shoot domain,
(b) the 3-way bulb domain, using the placeholder n for the number of bulbs,
(c) the crossing the river domain, using the predicate symbol item/1 to represent the set of items.

8.4 Effects of Actions

The effect of moving a block to a new location can be expressed by the rule

$$
\texttt{holds(loc(B,L),T+1) :- occurs(move(B,L),T).} \tag{8.8}
$$

(the location of B at time $T + 1$ is L if B was moved to L between times T and $T + 1$).

The effects of actions in the turkey shoot domain can be expressed by three rules:

```
holds(state_of_gun(loaded),T+1)  :- occurs(load,T).
holds(state_of_gun(unloaded),T+1)  :- occurs(shoot,T).
holds(state_of_turkey(dead),T+1)  :- occurs(shoot,T).
```

In these examples, the values of fluents at time $T + 1$ are completely determined by the action performed between the times T and $T + 1$; they do not depend on the state in which that action was executed. The modification of turkey shoot described in Exercise 8.5 is different: the effect of shooting in that version depends on the state of the gun. For that modification, the last of the rules above will be replaced by the rule

```
holds(state_of_turkey(dead),T+1)  :- occurs(shoot,T),
                    holds(state_of_gun(loaded),T).
```

In the crossing the river domain, the location of the boat after crossing depends on where the boat was previously. The effects of actions in that domain can be described using the auxiliary predicate `opposite/2`, defined by the rule

```
opposite(left,right; right,left).
```

as follows:

```
holds(loc(boat,L1),T+1)  :- occurs(cross(_),T),
                              holds(loc(boat,L),T),
                              opposite(L,L1).
holds(loc(I,L1),T+1)  :- occurs(cross(I),T), item(I),
                          holds(loc(I,L),T),
                          opposite(L,L1).
```

Exercise 8.12 Describe the effects of actions in the 3-state bulb domain by one rule.

Program (8.1), (8.3)–(8.8) is close to being an adequate description of scenario (i) from Sect. 8.1, but it is not completely satisfactory. In fact, that program has no stable models. To understand why, consider the program obtained from it by removing constraint (8.7). That smaller program has one stable model, consisting of the atoms

```
block(a)   block(b)   block(c)
holds(loc(a,b),0)   holds(loc(b,table),0)
holds(loc(c,table),0)
occurs(move(a,c),0)
holds(loc(a,c),1)
occurs(move(b,a),1)
holds(loc(b,a),2)
```

In this model, blocks b and c are not assigned a location at time 1, and blocks a and c are not assigned a location at time 2. This fact explains why the program becomes inconsistent after adding a constraint that requires a unique location for each block.

A satisfactory encoding of scenario (i) would imply that at time 1 both b and c are on the table, because that is where they were at time 0. It would also imply that at time 2 block a is on top of c, and c is on the table, because that is where they were at time 1. Program (8.1), (8.3)–(8.8) specifies the location of a block after moving it, but it does not say that a block "inherits" its location from the previous time instant if it is not moved. This is why program (8.1), (8.3)–(8.8) is unsatisfactory.

This difficulty, known as *the frame problem*, is quite general. If the turkey is alive then it will remain alive after loading the gun; an encoding of the turkey shoot domain will not be adequate unless it allows us to draw this conclusion. If a bulb is off then it will be off after pulling the chain controlling another bulb. If an item is on the left bank then it will be still there after crossing the river with any other item in the boat. Generally, a fluent can be presumed to have the same value that it had before if there is no evidence to the contrary. This principle plays an important role in the theory of dynamic systems, and it is known as "the commonsense law of inertia."

In the blocks world, inertia can be expressed by the rule

```
holds (loc (B, L) , T+1)  :- holds (loc (B, L) , T) ,
                              not not holds (loc (B, L) , T+1) ,
                              T = 0..h-1.
```
$$(8.9)$$

(the location of a block at time $T + 1$ is L if it was L at time T and there is no evidence that it is not L at time $T + 1$). Note the use of two negations, next to each other, in the body. The first of them translates the English expression "there is no evidence" into the language of logic programming. It is followed by the negation of the atom in the head of the rule; this is the translation of the English expression "to the contrary."

Program (8.1), (8.3)–(8.9) has one stable model—the one that we expected:

```
block (a)    block (b)    block (c)
holds (loc (a, b) , 0)    holds (loc (b, table) , 0)
holds (loc (c, table) , 0)
occurs (move (a, c) , 0)
holds (loc (a, c) , 1)    holds (loc (b, table) , 1)
holds (loc (c, table) , 1)
occurs (move (b, a) , 1)
holds (loc (a, c) , 2)    holds (loc (b, a) , 2)
holds (loc (c, table) , 2)
```

Exercise 8.13 Express inertia by rules (a) for the turkey shoot domain, (b) for the 3-way bulb domain, (c) for the crossing the river domain.

Inertia can be expressed also by choice rules. For instance, the choice rule

```
{holds (loc (B, L) , T+1) }  :- holds (loc (B, L) , T) ,  T = 0..h-1.
```
$$(8.10)$$

can be used in place of (8.9). This is not surprising in view of the fact that any propositional rule of the form

$$F \leftarrow \neg\neg F \wedge G$$

is strongly equivalent to

$$F \vee \neg F \leftarrow G$$

(Exercise 6.5 on page 97).

Exercise 8.14 Rewrite the inertia rule from Exercise 8.13(b) as a choice rule.

8.5 Nonexecutable Actions

As discussed above, scenario (i) from Sect. 8.1 can be represented by program (8.1), (8.3)–(8.9). But an attempt to turn that program into an encoding of scenario (ii) by replacing rule (8.5) with

$$\texttt{occurs(move(b,c),1).} \qquad (8.11)$$

will be unsuccessful. The modified program has a unique stable model that includes the atoms `holds(loc(a,c),2)` and `holds(loc(b,c),2)`, among others. In other words, instead of predicting that moving a and then b onto the same block c is impossible, the program predicts a state in which a and b are both on top of c. But there is no such state, because blocks are assumed to be stacked one on top of another forming towers.

The assumption that two blocks cannot be located on top of the same block can be expressed by the constraint

$$\texttt{B1 = B2 :- holds(loc(B1,B),T),}$$
$$\texttt{holds(loc(B2,B),T), block(B).} \qquad (8.12)$$

If we add this constraint to program (8.1), (8.3)–(8.9), and after that replace (8.5) by (8.11), then we will get an adequate representation of scenario (ii): the modified program has no stable models.

Exercise 8.15 Constraint (8.12) will become unacceptable if we remove the atom `block(B)` from its body. Explain why.

Besides the requirement that blocks be stacked one on top of another forming towers, there are two other reasons why moving a block may be impossible. First, a block cannot be moved if there is another block on top of it (Sect. 8.1):

$$\texttt{:- occurs(move(B,L),T), holds(loc(\_,B),T).} \qquad (8.13)$$

Second, a block cannot be moved to its current location:

$$\texttt{:- occurs(move(B,L),T), holds(loc(B,L),T).} \qquad (8.14)$$

Constraints (8.12)–(8.14) describe all possible reasons why the action of moving a block onto another block or onto the table can be nonexecutable. Constraints (8.13) and (8.14) are stated in terms of *preconditions*—conditions on a state that must be satisfied before executing the action. According to the former, the block that we want to move should be clear. According to the latter, the location to which we want to move it should be different from its current location. Constraint (8.12), on the other hand, restricts the executability of actions implicitly. It is stated in terms of fluents, and does not even mention actions. But in combination with rule (8.8), which describes the effect of moving a block, constraint (8.12) entails that a block cannot be moved to a place that is currently occupied.

The assumption that a block can be placed on top of another block only if the latter is clear can be thought of as a precondition similar to (8.13) and (8.14), and a constraint expressing that precondition can be used instead of (8.12).

Exercise 8.16 Write a constraint expressing that precondition.

In Sect. 8.8 we will say more about the relationship between this precondition and constraint (8.12).

Exercise 8.17 In the turkey shoot domain, the action *shoot* can be executed only when the gun is loaded, and the action *load* only when it is not. Express these preconditions by constraints.

Exercise 8.18 In the crossing the river domain, an item can be taken to the other bank only when it is on the same bank as the boat. Express this precondition by a constraint.

8.6 Prediction

Listings 8.1 and 8.2 reproduce the prediction program presented in Sects. 8.4 and 8.5, slightly modified. The first listing comprises the general rules, which are applicable to any blocks world prediction problem; the second is the input describing scenario (i) from Sect. 8.1. The modification involves introducing the auxiliary predicates `init/1` and `final/1`. The former allows us to describe the initial state a little more concisely—compare facts (8.6) with Line 3 of Listing 8.2. The latter is used in the `show` directive at the end of Listing 8.1.

Note that there are no "achieved" comments in these programs. Comments of that kind are not particularly useful in encodings of dynamic domains.

Exercise 8.19 (a) Write a prediction program for the turkey shoot domain. (b) Initially, the gun is unloaded and the turkey is alive. Then we load the gun, shoot the turkey, and load the gun again. Describe this scenario as input for your prediction program. (c) Run CLINGO on your program with that input.

Exercise 8.20 (a) Write a prediction program for the 3-way bulb domain. (b) There are 10 bulbs, and all switches are initially in the high position. We pull all chains controlling the bulbs, one after the other. Describe this scenario as input for your prediction program. (c) Run CLINGO on your program with that input.

Exercise 8.21 (a) Write a prediction program for the crossing the river domain. (b) There are two items, *a* and *b*. Initially *a* and the boat are on the left bank, and *b* is on the right bank. We take *a* to the opposite bank. Describe this scenario as input for your prediction program. (c) Run CLINGO on your program with that input.

Listing 8.1 Prediction in the blocks world

```
1  % Predict the effect of executing a sequence of actions in
2  % the blocks world.
3
4  % input: set block/1 of blocks; length h of the sequence of
5  %        actions; set init/1 of atoms representing the
6  %        initial state; set occurs/2 of pairs (a,t) such
7  %        that action a is executed between times t and t+1.
8
9  % effects of actions
10 holds(loc(B,L),T+1) :- occurs(move(B,L),T).
11
12 % two blocks can't be located on top of the same block
13 B1 = B2 :- holds(loc(B1,B),T), holds(loc(B2,B),T), block(B).
14
15 % a block can't be moved unless it is clear
16 :- occurs(move(B,L),T), holds(loc(_,B),T).
17
18 % a block can't be moved to its current location
19 :- occurs(move(B,L),T), holds(loc(B,L),T).
20
21 % existence and uniqueness of value
22 :- #count{L : holds(loc(B,L),T)} != 1, block(B), T = 0..h.
23
24 % inertia
25 {holds(loc(B,L),T+1)} :- holds(loc(B,L),T), T = 0..h-1.
26
27 % relationship between holds/2, init/1, and final/1
28 holds(C,0) :- init(C).
29 final(C) :- holds(C,h).
30
31 #show final/1.
```

Listing 8.2 Input for the blocks world prediction program

```
1  block(a; b; c).
2  #const h=2.
3  init(loc(a,b); loc(b,table); loc(c,table)).
4  occurs(move(a,c),0; move(b,a),1).
```

8.7   Planning

Now we will consider the use of answer set programming for generating a plan of a given length, if it exists. Take, for instance, the problem of constructing a plan of length 2 for example (iii) from Sect. 8.1. This problem can be encoded by modifying the prediction program shown in Listings 8.1 and 8.2 as follows.

First, we replace Line 4 in Listing 8.2, which describes a specific sequence of actions, by rules allowing an arbitrary sequence of actions of length h:

```
action(move(B1,B2)) :-  block(B1), block(B2), B1 != B2.
action(move(B,table)) :- block(B).
{occurs(A,T) : action(A)} = 1 :- T = 0..h-1
```

These rules allow two kinds of actions in a plan: moving a block onto another block and moving a block onto the table. After this modification, the program will have many stable models: one per each sequence of 2 actions that can be executed starting in state S_7.

Exercise 8.22 How many stable models do you think the modified program has?

Now it remains to add a constraint eliminating "bad" choices of actions—those for which the goal of having b on top of c at the end is not satisfied:

```
:- not holds(loc(b,c),h).
```

Stable models of the new program represent all plans of length 2 that solve the problem in question.

Exercise 8.23 How many stable models do you think are eliminated by adding this constraint?

A general planning program for the blocks world and an input file for it that represents problem (iii) from Sect. 8.1 are shown in Listings 8.3 and 8.4. The auxiliary predicate goal/1 is used to encode the goal of the planning problem.

Exercise 8.24 In the blocks world with 9 blocks, the initial state is

$$
\begin{array}{lll}
1 & & \\
2 & 5 & \\
3 & 6 & 8 \\
4 & 7 & 9
\end{array}
\qquad (8.15)
$$

and the goal is to have 9 on top of 6, 6 on top of 3, and 3 on the table. We would like to achieve this goal in 7 steps. (a) Encode this problem as an input file for the blocks world planning program in Listing 8.3. (b) Use CLINGO to find a solution.

If a blocks world planning program does not have stable models for a given input then we can conclude that there is no plan of required length h. It does not follow, generally, that there is no plan of length strictly less than h, so that we cannot

Listing 8.3 Planning in the blocks world

```
1   % For a planning problem in the blocks world, find solutions
2   % of a given length.
3
4   % input: set block/1 of blocks; set init/1 of atoms
5   %          representing the initial state; set goal/1 of atoms
6   %          representing the goal; length h of solutions.
7
8   % choice of actions
9   action(move(B1,B2)) :-  block(B1), block(B2), B1 != B2.
10  action(move(B,table)) :- block(B).
11  {occurs(A,T) : action(A)} = 1 :- T = 0..h-1.
12
13  % effects of actions
14  holds(loc(B,L),T+1) :- occurs(move(B,L),T).
15
16  % two blocks can't be located on top of the same block
17  B1 = B2 :- holds(loc(B1,B),T), holds(loc(B2,B),T), block(B).
18
19  % a block can't be moved unless it is clear
20  :- occurs(move(B,L),T), holds(loc(_,B),T).
21
22  % a block can't be moved to its current location
23  :- occurs(move(B,L),T), holds(loc(B,L),T).
24
25  % existence and uniqueness of value
26  :- #count{L : holds(loc(B,L),T)} != 1, block(B), T = 0..h.
27
28  % inertia
29  {holds(loc(B,L),T+1)} :- holds(loc(B,L),T), T = 0..h-1.
30
31  % relationship between holds/2, init/1, and goal/1.
32  holds(C,0) :- init(C).
33  :- goal(C), not holds(C,h).
34
35  #show occurs/2.
```

Listing 8.4 Input for the blocks world planning program

```
1   block(a; b; c).
2   init(loc(a,b) ; loc(b,table) ; loc(c,table)).
3   goal(loc(b,c)).
4   #const h=2.
```

conclude that the given value of h is too small. But it is easy to find out whether it is indeed necessary to increase h. This can be accomplished by introducing a new action, which has no effect on the values of fluents:

$$\texttt{action(wait).} \tag{8.16}$$

Allowing this trivial action to appear in the plan is essentially equivalent to allowing h to be replaced by a smaller number.

Furthermore, if we know a value of h such that the planning program with line (8.16) added to the input has a stable model then we can instruct CLINGO to look for the shortest possible solution to the given problem. To do that, add a directive that calls for using the trivial action as often as possible—

$$\texttt{\#maximize\{1,T : occurs(wait,T)\}.}$$
$$\text{or} \tag{8.17}$$
$$\texttt{\#maximize\{T : occurs(wait,T)\}.}$$

(see the discussion of the chromatic number example in Sect. 7.4). Take, for example, the input shown in the solution to Exercise 8.24, replace the value 7 of the placeholder h by a larger number—say, 10—and add to it line (8.16) and the second of directives (8.17). For the modified input, the last part of the output produced by CLINGO may look like this:

```
Answer: 5
occurs(move(1,table),0) occurs(move(2,1),1)
occurs(move(8,table),2) occurs(move(3,table),3)
occurs(move(5,2),4) occurs(move(6,3),5)
occurs(move(9,6),6) occurs(wait,7) occurs(wait,8)
occurs(wait,9)
Optimization: -24
OPTIMUM FOUND
```

The fact that 3 out of the 10 occurs atoms in the optimal stable model contain the trivial action shows that the length of the shortest solution to the given planning problem is 7. One of these solutions is given by the occurs atoms that do not contain wait.

Exercise 8.25 (a) Write a planning program for the turkey shoot domain. (b) Initially, the gun is loaded and the turkey is alive. We would like the gun to be loaded while the turkey is dead. Use CLINGO to solve this planning problem.

Exercise 8.26 (a) Write a planning program for the 3-way bulb domain. (b) There are 3 bulbs, and initially all switches are in the medium position. We would like all of them to be off. Use CLINGO to solve this planning problem.

In some cases, we want to find a solution to a planning problem that satisfies some additional conditions, beyond those expressed by the definition of `goal/1`. This can be often accomplished by adding constraints to the input of the planning program. As an example, consider the planning problem from Exercise 8.24 with the additional requirement: there should never be more than 3 towers on the table while the plan is executed. (The table is small, and there is no room on it for more than 3 blocks side by side.) This requirement can be expressed by the constraint

```
:- #count{B : holds(loc(B,table),T)} > 3, T = 0..h.
```

Exercise 8.27 Use CLINGO to find the shortest plan satisfying this condition.

Exercise 8.28 (a) Write a planning program for the crossing the river domain. (b) In the fox, goose and bag of beans puzzle, a farmer must transport a fox, goose and bag of beans from one side of a river to another using a boat which can only hold one item in addition to the farmer, subject to the constraints that the fox cannot be left alone with the goose, and the goose cannot be left alone with the beans. This puzzle can be viewed as a planning problem in the crossing the river domain with additional conditions. Write an input file for your crossing the river program that represents this puzzle. (c) Use CLINGO to solve the puzzle.

Exercise 8.29 The 15-puzzle consists of square tiles numbered from 1 to 15 placed in a 4-by-4 box:

3	6	9	12
4	13	10	7
	5	8	14
15	1	7	2

The player can slide tiles, one at a time, into the vacant position. In the configuration above, for instance, any of the tiles 4, 5, 15 can be moved.

Write a planning program for this domain.

Exercise 8.30 The Tower of Hanoi puzzle consists of three pegs and a number of disks of different sizes, which can slide onto any peg. Initially the disks are in ascending order of size on one peg, the smallest at the top. The goal is to move the entire stack to another peg, obeying the following rules:

- Only one disk can be moved at a time.
- Each move consists of taking the upper disk from one of the pegs and placing it on top of another peg.
- No larger disk may be placed on top of a smaller disk.

The minimal number of moves required to solve a Tower of Hanoi puzzle is known to be $2^n - 1$, where n is the number of disks.

Write a planning program for this domain.

8.8   Concurrency

A robot with several grippers may be able to move several objects simultaneously. Think, for instance, of a robot with two grippers facing blocks world configuration (8.15) on page 140. Instead of choosing between the actions, say, *move*(1,*table*) and *move*(5,*table*), it can execute these actions concurrently. Or it can swap blocks 1 and 5 by executing the actions *move*(1,6) and *move*(5,2). These two actions can only be performed concurrently; any one of them is not executable in state (8.15) by itself.

To talk about the concurrent execution of actions in terms of transition diagrams, we need to modify the description of that concept given in Sect. 8.2 and label the edges of the graph by sets of actions, rather than individual actions. In case of the blocks world with 3 blocks (Fig. 8.2, page 130) and a robot with 2 grippers, every edge will be labeled by a set consisting of 1 or 2 actions. Let us assume that the robot is unable to move a block onto a block that is being moved at the same time. Under this assumption, instead of the edges (8.2) starting at S_7 (page 131), in the modified transition diagram we will see

> edge labeled $\{move(a, c)\}$ leading to S_9,
> edge labeled $\{move(a, table)\}$ leading to S_{13},
> edge labeled $\{move(c, a)\}$ leading to S_4,
> edge labeled $\{move(a, table), move(c, b)\}$ leading to S_{12}.

To encode the assumption that blocks are being moved by a robot with m grippers (or by m agents whose actions are synchronous), we replace Line 12 in Listing 8.3 by the rule

```
1 {occurs(A,T) : action(A)} m :- T = 0..h-1.
```

The assumption that the destination of a move is not moving concurrently can be expressed by the constraint

```
:- occurs(move(_,B),T), occurs(move(B,_),T).
```

It is interesting that constraint (8.12) and the precondition from Exercise 8.16 (page 138) are not interchangeable when concurrent actions are allowed. The latter would not allow B1 to be moved onto B2 even while the block covering B2 is being moved away. For instance, it would prohibit swapping blocks 1 and 5 in state (8.15). This is much too strong. On the other hand, it would allow two blocks to be moved concurrently onto the same block that is currently clear. For instance, it would allow moving blocks 1 and 5 onto block 8 concurrently. In this sense, it is too weak. Constraint (8.12), which restricts the executability of actions indirectly, does not suffer from these problems.

When concurrent actions are allowed, the shortest solution to a planning problem is not necessarily the most economical in the sense of the total number of actions: counting actions is different from counting steps.

The use of rule (8.16) and directive (8.17) for generating the shortest solution to a planning problem of this kind requires an additional constraint: the trivial action is not executed concurrently with any other action. This can be written as

```
A = wait :- occurs(wait,T), occurs(A,T).
```

Exercise 8.31 Use CLINGO to find out how many steps a robot with 2 grippers would need to solve the planning problem from Exercise 8.24.

Exercise 8.32 (a) Modify the planning program from Exercise 8.26(a) to reflect the assumption that the person operating the switches uses both hands and can access any two switches simultaneously. (b) How many steps do you think are needed to solve the planning problem from Exercise 8.26(b) under this assumption? Use CLINGO to verify your conjecture.

8.9 Bibliographical and Historical Remarks

The idea of declarative planning goes back to 1959 [90]. The first system capable of producing plans from action descriptions, based on resolution theorem proving [108], was designed 10 years later [59]. Around the same time, the term "fluent" was introduced, and the frame problem was identified [94]. Further work on declarative planning involved the design of specialized logic-based languages for describing effects of actions [39, 54, 103].

For many years, the frame problem was considered a difficult, unsolved problem in knowledge representation. It was part of the motivation behind the study of nonmonotonic reasoning, and it became an active research area since 1986, after the publication of a counterexample [60, 61] showing that an attempt to solve the frame problem using circumscription [92] was unsatisfactory.

An early statement expressing the commonsense law of inertia can be found in Leibniz's *Introduction to a Secret Encyclopedia*: "Everything is presumed to remain in the state in which it is" [74]. A successful formalization of that idea in the language of logic programming proposed in 1992 [54] was similar to the "frame default" suggested as an approach to the frame problem in 1980 [80, 107]. The choice rule formulation used in this chapter was invented in 2012 [11].

The 15-puzzle was invented in 1880 by Noyes Chapman. The Tower of Hanoi puzzle was invented in 1883 by Édouard Lucas.

The possibility of using satisfiability solvers for planning was demonstrated in 1992 [70]. The relationship between planning and stable models was discussed in a paper published in 1995 [115], and an answer set solver was first used for planning in 1997 [28].

A few years later, the answer set programming approach to planning was used in a decision support system for the Space Shuttle [100], called the RCS/USA Advisor. (In this case, USA stands for "United Space Alliance," the name of a spaceflight operation company). In view of the importance of that project in the early history of answer set programming, we will talk about it in some detail.

The Space Shuttle program was a NASA spaceflight program that accomplished transportation for crew and cargo from 1981 to 2011. Maneuvering the Space Shuttle in space was controlled by its Reaction Control System (RCS), which consists of fuel and oxidizer tanks and the plumbing that provides propellant to the maneuvering jets. The RCS includes also the electronic circuitry that controls the valves in the fuel lines and prepares the jets for receiving firing commands.

The RCS was computer controlled during takeoff and landing. While in orbit, astronauts controlled the RCS by flipping switches that open or close valves and energize circuitry. In extreme circumstances, such as a faulty switch, astronauts would communicate the problem to the ground flight controllers, who come up with a sequence of computer commands to perform the desired task.

It represented the RCS as a dynamic system similar to the examples in this chapter. For instance, the state of a switch was treated as a fluent with three values: *open*, *closed*, and *gpc* ("controlled by General Purpose Computers"). The effect of flipping a switch can be expressed by the rule

```
holds(in_state(Sw,S),T+1)  :- occurs(flip(Sw,S),T).
```
$$\text{(8.18)}$$
similar to rule (8.8) on page 134 that describes the effect of moving a block.

The description of flipping a switch in the RCS/USA Advisor is actually more elaborate than (8.18); it takes into account the fact that a switch can be faulty:

```
holds(in_state(Sw,S),T+1)  :- occurs(flip(Sw,S),T),

                              not stuck(Sw).       (8.19)
```

This feature is essential, because the program was supposed to produce workable plans even when some switches malfunction.

Other rules of the program describe the relationship between the state of a switch and the state of the valve that it controls; between the pressure on a jet and the states of the valves separating it from fuel and oxidizer tanks; and so forth. In combination with rule (8.19), these rules describe remote, indirect effects of flipping a switch. The bodies of these additional rules do not refer to executing actions. But they are similar to the body of rule (8.19) in the sense that they include conditions restricting them to "normal" cases, when the valves are not stuck and not leaking.

The RCS consists of three subsystems: left, right, and forward. The RCS/USA Advisor uses the atom `action_of(A,R)` ("A is an action of subsystem R) instead of `action(A)` that we saw in the blocks world planning program (Listing 8.3 on page 141). Instead of the rule on Line 11 of that program, which allows one action at each time instant, the RCS/USA Advisor program allows up to three actions to be executed concurrently—at most one for each subsystem.

Chapter 9
Conclusion

The discussion of answer set programming in this book is incomplete in three ways. First, it says almost nothing about the algorithms that answer set solvers use to find stable models, about what happens "under the hood." Section 3.4 is, in fact, the only place where the operation of answer set solvers is discussed in any detail. The algorithms implemented in SMODELS are described in Chaps. 3 and 4 of the doctoral dissertation of one of its designers [112]. You can learn about the operation of CLINGO from Chaps. 4 and 6 of the book [45] written by members of the Potassco team.

Second, there are several useful answer set programming constructs that we did not have a chance to mention. Some of them are available in the language of CLINGO—conditional literals, external functions, and multi-shot solving. They are described in the Potassco User Guide, which can be downloaded from the website of the Potassco project, https://potassco.org. One other interesting construct, intensional functions, is motivated by the fact that ASP definitions of functions are somewhat cumbersome. Compare, for instance, the definition of the predicate fac/2 in lines 5 and 6 of Listing 2.6 (page 19) with the definition of factorial in Haskell (page 2). Incorporating intensional functions is an attempt to overcome this defect by merging ASP with functional programming [6, 11, 17]. We did not talk about the use of external information sources [29], about rules with ordered disjunction [14], ASP with sorts [4], ASP with consistency-restoring rules [5, 7], constraint ASP [8, 9, 47, 67], ASP with preferences [15], and probabilistic ASP [21].

Third, most examples of programs here are "toy examples" chosen for the purpose of illustrating the possibilities of the language. Serious applications of answer set programming are discussed in recent surveys [31, 36], and studying them will help the reader appreciate the value of the programming paradigm described in this book.

© Springer Nature Switzerland AG 2019
V. Lifschitz, *Answer Set Programming*,
https://doi.org/10.1007/978-3-030-24658-7_9

Appendix A
Answers to Exercises

Answers to some of the exercises can be verified by running CLINGO, and they are not included here.

2.1. (c) Replace rule (1.1) by `large(C) :- size(C,S), S > 500.`

2.2. (a) *X* is a child of *Y* if *Y* is a parent of *X*.

2.3. (a) `large(germany) :- size(germany,83), size(uk,64),`
`                            83 > 64.`
(b) `child(dan,bob) :- parent(bob,dan).`

2.4. (b), (c), and (d).

2.5. `parent(ann,bob; bob,carol; bob,dan).`

2.8. `p(0,0*0+0+41) :- 0 = 0..3.`

2.10. `p(2**N,2**(N+1)) :- N = 0..3.`

2.11. (a) `p(N, (-1)**N) :- N = 0..4.`
(b) `p(M,N) :- M = 1..4, N = 1..4, M >= N.`

2.12. (a) `grandparent(X,Z) :- parent(X,Y), parent(Y,Z).`

2.13. (a) `sibling(X,Y) :- parent(Z,X), parent(Z,Y), X != Y.`

2.14. `enrolled(S) :- enrolled(S,C).`

2.15. `same_city(X,Y) :- lives_in(X,C), lives_in(Y,C),`
`                        X != Y.`

2.16. `older(X,Y) :- age(X,M), age(Y,N), M > N.`

2.18.
Line 5: `noncoprime(N) :- N = 1..n, I = 2..N, N\I = 0,`
`                    k\I = 0.`
Line 10: `coprime(N) :- N = 1..n, not noncoprime(N).`

© Springer Nature Switzerland AG 2019
V. Lifschitz, *Answer Set Programming*,
https://doi.org/10.1007/978-3-030-24658-7

2.19.
Line 6:

```
three(N) :- N = 1..n, I = 0..n, J = 0..n, K = 0..n,
            N = I**2+J**2+K**2.
```

(See Sect. 3.4 for alternative definitions of `three/1`.)

Line 11: `more_than_three(N) :- N = 1..n, not three(N).`

2.22. (a) {p(a)}. (b) p(a). (c) {p(a)}.

2.24. (a) {q(a,a; a,b; b,a; b,b)} = 1.

2.25. (a) 1 {r(a,Y; b,Y)} :- q(Y).

2.27.

```
{p(a);q(b)}.
:- not p(a), not q(b).
```

3.1. (a) n^n. (b) $n!$. (c) $n!$.

3.2.
Line 15: `T1 = T2 :- at(G,T1), at(G,T2).`
Line 18: `T1 = T2 :- like(G1,G2), at(G1,T1), at(G2,T2).`
Line 21: `:- dislike(G1,G2), at(G1,T), at(G2,T).`

3.4. Numbers 1 and 2 cannot be included in the same set, because $1 + 1 = 2$. Denote the set containing 1 by A, and the set containing 2 by B. Number 4 cannot belong to B, because $2 + 2 = 4$. It follows that 4 belongs to A. Then 3 cannot belong to A, because $1 + 3 = 4$. It follows that 3 belongs to B. But then 5 can belong neither to A $(1 + 4 = 5)$ nor to B $(2 + 3 = 5)$; contradiction.

3.5. {1, 3, 8}, {2, 9, 10}, {4, 5, 6, 7}.

3.7. r^n.

3.8. Replace Line 10 by `I = J :- in(I,K), in(J,K), in(I+J,K).`

3.10. `:- in(I,K), in(J,K), I < J, in(2*J-I,K).`

3.11.
Line 13: `I = J :- in(I), in(J), s(X,I), s(X,J).`
Line 16: `covered(X) :- in(I), s(X,I).`
Line 19: `:- s(X,_), not covered(X).`

3.12.
Line 6: `{in(X) : vertex(X)} = n.`
Line 9: `covered(X,Y) :- edge(X,Y), in(X).`
Line 10: `covered(X,Y) :- edge(X,Y), in(Y).`
Line 14: `:- edge(X,Y), not covered(X,Y).`

3.13.
Line 8: `{color(X,C) : color(C)} = 1 :- vertex(X).`
Line 12: `:- edge(X,Y), color(X,C), color(Y,C).`

3.14. (a) $n^{2(n^2-k)}$. (b) $(n^2 - k)!$.

4.1. Only one: $\{q, r\}$.

4.2. $\neg p \vee \neg q$.

4.3. $\emptyset, \{q\}, \{r\}, \{p, q, r\}$.

4.4. $\emptyset, \{p, q, r, s\}$.

4.5.

(a) A subset of $\{p_1, p_2, \dots, p_8\}$ satisfies $p_1 \wedge p_2$ iff it includes both p_1 and p_2. For each of the other 6 atomic propositions we can decide arbitrarily whether to include it. Consequently the number of models of $p_1 \wedge p_2$ is 2^6, or 64.

(b) The set $\{p_1, p_2, \dots, p_8\}$ has 2^8 subsets. A subset of that set satisfies $p_1 \leftarrow p_2$ unless it includes p_2 but does not include p_1. The number of such exceptional subsets is 2^6. It follows that the number of models of $p_1 \leftarrow p_2$ is $2^8 - 2^6$, or 192.

4.6. (a) $\{p_1, p_3, p_5, \dots\}$ and $\{p_0, p_1, p_3, p_5, \dots\}$. (b) $\emptyset, \{p_0\}, \{p_0, p_1\}$.

4.7. (a): not equivalent; for example, $\{q\}$ satisfies $p \leftarrow r$ but does not satisfy the first of the formulas $p \leftarrow q, q \leftarrow r$. (b)–(e): equivalent.

4.8. (a) $\top$. (b) $p \vee q$. (c) $p \leftarrow q$.

4.9. (a) p. (b) $\{\neg p, q \leftarrow r\}$.

4.10. Both (a) and (b).

4.11. $q \leftarrow p$.

4.12. This set is equivalent to $\{p \leftrightarrow q, q \leftarrow q \wedge r\}$. Since the second formula is a tautology, it can be dropped.

4.13. (a) $\{p, r\}, \{q, s\}, \{p, r, s\}, \{q, r, s\}, \{p, q, r, s\}$. (b) $\{p, r\}$ and $\{q, s\}$.

4.14. $\{p, q\}$ and $\{r\}$. Note that $\{p, q\}$ is a minimal model even though it has more elements than $\{r\}$.

4.15. (a) All interpretations are models. (b) The only minimal model is $\emptyset$.

4.16. (a) All sets of interpretations containing Γ are models. (b) The only minimal model is Γ itself.

4.17. $p \vee q \vee r \vee s$.

4.18. $p \leftarrow q$ and $q \leftarrow p$.

4.19. Step 1: include r_1; step 2: add q_1; step 3: add p_1 and p_2. Minimal model: $\{p_1, p_2, q_1, r_1\}$.

4.20. (a) Minimal model: $\emptyset$. (b) Step 1: include p_5. Minimal model: $\{p_5\}$. (c) Step 1: include p_5 and p_6; step 2: add p_4; step 3: add p_3; step 4: add p_2; step 5: add p_1. Minimal model: $\{p_1, \dots, p_6\}$.

4.21. $p \leftarrow \neg q$.

4.22. (a) Step 1: include p_3; step 2: add p_2; step 3: add p_1. Minimal model: $\{p_1, p_2, p_3\}$. (b) Step 1: include p_3; step 2: add p_4; step 3: add p_5; and so on. Minimal model: $\{p_3, p_4, \dots\}$.

4.23. (a)

```
p.
q :- p, r.
r :- p.
r :- t.
s :- r, t.
```

4.24. (a)

```
p1 :- q1.
p2 :- q1.
p1 :- q2.
p2 :- q2.
q1 :- r1.
q1 :- r2.
r1.
```

4.26.

(a)

$$
\begin{aligned}
&p(0, 1), \\
&p(1, 2), \\
&q(v_1, v_2) \leftarrow p(v_1, v_2) \wedge \top \wedge \top \quad \text{for all } v_1, v_2 \in \mathbf{S} \cup \mathbf{Z} \text{ such that } v_1, v_2 > 0, \\
&q(v_1, v_2) \leftarrow p(v_1, v_2) \wedge \bot \wedge \top \quad \text{for all } v_1, v_2 \in \mathbf{S} \cup \mathbf{Z} \text{ such that } v_1 \leq 0, \ v_2 > 0, \\
&q(v_1, v_2) \leftarrow p(v_1, v_2) \wedge \top \wedge \bot \quad \text{for all } v_1, v_2 \in \mathbf{S} \cup \mathbf{Z} \text{ such that } v_1 > 0, \ v_2 \leq 0, \\
&q(v_1, v_2) \leftarrow p(v_1, v_2) \wedge \bot \wedge \bot \quad \text{for all } v_1, v_2 \in \mathbf{S} \cup \mathbf{Z} \text{ such that } v_1, v_2 \leq 0.
\end{aligned}
$$

(b)

$$
\begin{aligned}
&p(0, 1), \\
&p(1, 2), \\
&q(v_1, v_2) \leftarrow p(v_1, v_2) \quad \text{for all } v_1, v_2 \in \mathbf{S} \cup \mathbf{Z} \text{ such that } v_1, v_2 > 0.
\end{aligned}
$$

(c) Step 1: include $p(0, 1)$ and $p(1, 2)$. Step 2: add $q(1, 2)$.

4.27.

(a)

$$parent(ann, bob),$$
$$parent(bob, carol),$$
$$parent(bob, dan),$$

$child(v_1, v_2) \leftarrow parent(v_2, v_1)$ for all $v_1, v_2 \in \mathbf{S} \cup \mathbf{Z}$,

$ancestor(v_1, v_2) \leftarrow parent(v_1, v_2)$ for all $v_1, v_2 \in \mathbf{S} \cup \mathbf{Z}$,

$ancestor(v_1, v_3) \leftarrow ancestor(v_1, v_2)$

$\wedge \; ancestor(v_2, v_3)$ for all $v_1, v_2, v_3 \in \mathbf{S} \cup \mathbf{Z}$.

(b) Step 1: include

$$parent(ann, bob), \; parent(bob, carol), \; parent(bob, dan).$$

Step 2: add

$$child(bob, ann), \; child(carol, bob), \; child(dan, bob),$$
$$ancestor(ann, bob), \; ancestor(bob, carol), \; ancestor(bob, dan).$$

Step 3: add

$$ancestor(ann, carol), ancestor(ann, dan).$$

4.28.

(a)

$$p(1) \vee p(2) \vee p(3),$$
$$\perp \leftarrow p(v) \wedge \top \quad \text{for all } v \in \mathbf{S} \cup \mathbf{Z} \text{ such that } v > 2,$$
$$\perp \leftarrow p(v) \wedge \perp \quad \text{for all } v \in \mathbf{S} \cup \mathbf{Z} \text{ such that } v \leq 2.$$

(b) The formulas in the second line can be equivalently rewritten as $\neg p(v)$, and the formulas in the last line are tautologies. It follows this set of formulas is equivalent to

$$p(1) \vee p(2) \vee p(3),$$
$$\neg p(v) \qquad \qquad \text{for all } v \in \mathbf{S} \cup \mathbf{Z} \text{ such that } v > 2.$$

(A.1)

Since the set of formulas in the second line includes $\neg p(3)$, the formula in the first line can be equivalently replaced by $p(1) \vee p(2)$. (c) Set (A.1) has two minimal models, $\{p(1)\}$ and $\{p(2)\}$.

4.29.

(a)

$$p(a),$$
$$q(v_1, v_2) \leftarrow p(v_1) \qquad \text{for all } v_1, v_2 \in \mathbf{S} \cup \mathbf{Z}.$$

(b) Step 1: include $p(a)$. Step 2: Add $q(a, v)$ for all $v \in \mathbf{S} \cup \mathbf{Z}$.

4.30. (a) and (b).

4.31. $4, 6, 8, 9, 12, 16$.

4.32. (a) $3**(0..2)$; (b) $10*(2..4)+2$.

4.33. (a) $square(1, 1) \wedge square(1, 2) \wedge square(2, 1) \wedge square(2, 2)$.
(b) $q \leftarrow square(1, 1) \vee square(1, 2) \vee square(2, 1) \vee square(2, 2)$. (c) $\top$. (d) $q \leftarrow \bot$.
Tautologies: (c) and (d).

4.34. (a) $\{p(1),\ q \leftarrow p(1) \vee p(2) \vee p(3)\}$. (b) $\{p(1), q\}$.

4.35.

(a)

$$\top \leftarrow \top,$$
$$p(1) \leftarrow \top,$$
$$\top \leftarrow \bot.$$

(b) $\{p(1)\}$.

4.36.

(a)

$$p(1) \wedge p(2) \wedge p(3),$$
$$q(2) \leftarrow p(2) \wedge \top,$$
$$q(3) \leftarrow p(3) \wedge \top,$$
$$q(4) \leftarrow p(4) \wedge \top,$$
$$q(v) \leftarrow p(v) \wedge \bot \qquad \text{for all } v \in \mathbf{S} \cup \mathbf{Z} \setminus \{2, 3, 4\}.$$

(b)

$$p(1) \wedge p(2) \wedge p(3),$$
$$q(2) \leftarrow p(2),$$
$$q(3) \leftarrow p(3),$$
$$q(4) \leftarrow p(4).$$

(c) Step 1: include $p(1)$, $p(2)$, $p(3)$. Step 2: add $q(2)$ and $q(3)$.

4.37.

(a)

$$p(1, 1) \land p(1, 2),$$
$$q(v_1, v_2) \leftarrow p(v_1, v_2) \land \top \quad \text{for all } v_1, v_2 \in \mathbf{S} \cup \mathbf{Z} \text{ such that } v_1 \neq v_2,$$
$$q(v, v) \leftarrow p(v, v) \land \bot \quad \text{for all } v \in \mathbf{S} \cup \mathbf{Z},$$
$$q(v_1, v_2) \leftarrow q(v_2, v_1) \quad \text{for all } v_1, v_2 \in \mathbf{S} \cup \mathbf{Z}.$$

(b)

$$p(1, 1) \land p(1, 2),$$
$$q(v_1, v_2) \leftarrow p(v_1, v_2) \quad \text{for all } v_1, v_2 \in \mathbf{S} \cup \mathbf{Z} \text{ such that } v_1 \neq v_2,$$
$$q(v_1, v_2) \leftarrow q(v_2, v_1) \quad \text{for all } v_1, v_2 \in \mathbf{S} \cup \mathbf{Z}.$$

(c) Step 1: include $p(1, 1)$, $p(1, 2)$. Step 2: add $q(1, 2)$. Step 3: add $q(2, 1)$.

4.38.

(a)

$$p(1) \land p(2) \land p(3),$$
$$q(i) \land q(n) \land q(j) \leftarrow p(n) \quad \text{for all } n \in \mathbf{Z},$$
$$\top \leftarrow p(v) \quad \text{for all } v \in \mathbf{S}.$$

where i, j are the values of $n - 1$, $n + 1$,
(b) The rules in the last line are tautologies and can be dropped.
(c) Step 1: include $p(1)$, $p(2)$, $p(3)$. Step 2: add $q(0)$, $q(1)$, $q(2)$, $q(3)$, $q(4)$.

4.39.

(a)

$$p(1) \land p(2) \land p(3),$$
$$\top \leftarrow p(1),$$
$$\bot \leftarrow p(v) \quad \text{for all } v \in \mathbf{S} \cup \mathbf{Z} \setminus \{1\}.$$

(b) Since the set of formulas in the last line includes $\bot \leftarrow p(2)$, the propositional image has no models.

4.40.

(a)

$$p(1),$$
$$q(n) \leftarrow p(m) \quad \text{for all } n \in \mathbf{Z}, \text{ where } m \text{ is the value of } (-1)^n,$$
$$q(v) \leftarrow \bot \quad \text{for all } v \in \mathbf{S}.$$

(b) Step 1: Include $p(1)$. Step 2: Add $q(n)$ for all even numbers n.

5.1. (a) The reduct of the program relative to $\{p, q, r\}$ is

$$
\begin{aligned}
&p, \\
&q, \\
&r \leftarrow p \wedge \top.
\end{aligned}
\tag{A.2}
$$

and the only minimal model of the reduct is $\{p, q, r\}$. (b) Take any interpretation I different from $\{p, q, r\}$, and consider two cases. *Case 1:* $s \in I$. The reduct of the program relative to I is

$$
\begin{aligned}
&p, \\
&q, \\
&r \leftarrow p \wedge \bot.
\end{aligned}
$$

Its minimal model $\{p, q\}$ does not contain s. Consequently it is different from I. *Case 2:* $s \notin I$. The reduct is (A.2), and its only minimal model $\{p, q, r\}$ is different from I.

5.2. (a) Take any interpretation I, and consider two cases. *Case 1:* $p \in I$. The reduct is $p \leftarrow \bot$. This is a tautology, so that its only minimal model is empty. It does not satisfy the condition characterizing Case 1. *Case 2:* $p \notin I$. The reduct is $p \leftarrow \top$, and its minimal model $\{p\}$ does not satisfy the condition characterizing Case 2. Consequently the given program has no stable models.

5.3. (a) Take any interpretation I, and consider two cases. *Case 1:* $q \in I$. The reduct is

$$
\begin{aligned}
&p \vee q, \\
&\bot \leftarrow p \wedge \bot.
\end{aligned}
$$

The second line is a tautology, so that the minimal models of the reduct are the minimal models of its first rule, $\{p\}$ and $\{q\}$. The latter satisfies the condition characterizing Case 1, so that it is a stable model of the given program. *Case 2:* $q \notin I$. The reduct is

$$
\begin{aligned}
&p \vee q, \\
&\bot \leftarrow p \wedge \top.
\end{aligned}
$$

The second rule is equivalent to $\neg p$, so that the reduct is equivalent to $\{q, \neg p\}$. The minimal model $\{q\}$ of the reduct does not satisfy the condition characterizing this case. Consequently $\{q\}$ is the only stable model of the given program.

5.4. (a) Take any interpretation I, and consider four cases. *Case 1: $p, q \in I$.* The reduct is

$$p \leftarrow \bot,$$
$$q \leftarrow \bot,$$
$$p \leftarrow q,$$
$$q \leftarrow p.$$

The minimal model $\emptyset$ does not satisfy the condition characterizing this case. *Case 2: $p \in I, q \notin I$.* The reduct is

$$p \leftarrow \top,$$
$$q \leftarrow \bot,$$
$$p \leftarrow q,$$
$$q \leftarrow p.$$

The minimal model $\{p, q\}$ does not satisfy the condition characterizing this case. *Case 3: $p \notin I, q \in I$.* A similar calculation leads to the same result. *Case 4: $p, q \notin I$.* The reduct is

$$p \leftarrow \top,$$
$$q \leftarrow \top,$$
$$p \leftarrow q,$$
$$q \leftarrow p.$$

The minimal model $\{p, q\}$ does not satisfy the condition characterizing this case. Consequently the given program has no stable models.

5.5.

(a)

I	Reduct relative to I	$s(I)$	Fixpoint?
$\emptyset$	$\{q \leftarrow \top\}$	$\{q\}$	
$\{p\}$	$\{q \leftarrow \bot\}$	$\emptyset$	
$\{q\}$	$\{q \leftarrow \top\}$	$\{q\}$	✓
$\{p, q\}$	$\{q \leftarrow \bot\}$	$\emptyset$	

(b)

I	Reduct relative to I	$s(I)$	Fixpoint?
$\emptyset$	$\{p \leftarrow \bot\}$	$\emptyset$	✓
$\{p\}$	$\{p \leftarrow \top\}$	$\{p\}$	✓

5.6. For every subset I of $\{p, q, r, s, t\}$, $s(I) = \{p, q, r\}$.

5.7.

(a) The program can be rewritten as

$$p,$$
$$q \leftarrow \top,$$
$$r \leftarrow \neg q$$

(Theorem on Facts),

$$p,$$
$$q,$$
$$r \leftarrow \neg q$$

(Table 4.1),

$$p,$$
$$q,$$
$$r \leftarrow \neg \top$$

(Theorem on Facts), and finally as

$$p,$$
$$q$$

(Table 4.1). We conclude that $\{p, q\}$ is the only stable model of the given program.

(b) The program can be rewritten as

$$p,$$
$$q \vee r \leftarrow \top,$$
$$s \vee t \leftarrow \neg \top$$

(Theorem on Facts), and then as

$$p,$$
$$q \vee r$$

(Table 4.1). The minimal models $\{p, q\}$ and $\{p, r\}$ of this positive program are the stable models of the given program.

5.8.

(a) The program can be rewritten as

$$p,$$
$$q,$$
$$r \leftarrow p \wedge \neg \bot,$$

and, using Table 4.1, as the definite program

$$p,$$
$$q,$$
$$r \leftarrow p.$$

The minimal model of this program is $\{p, q, r\}$.
(b) The program can be rewritten as

$$p \leftarrow \neg q,$$
$$q \leftarrow \neg p \wedge \bot.$$

Transformations from Table 4.1 allow us to drop the second rule. Since q is irrelevant for the remaining rule, that rule can be rewritten as p. The only stable model of the given program is $\{p\}$.

5.9. (a)–(c): $q \leftarrow \bot$. (d)–(f): $\top \leftarrow q$.

5.10.

(a)

$$p(5) \wedge p(6) \wedge p(7),$$
$$q(n) \leftarrow \top \wedge \neg p(n) \qquad (n = 1, \ldots, 5),$$
$$q(v) \leftarrow \bot \wedge \neg p(v) \qquad \text{for all } v \text{ other than } 1, \ldots, 5.$$

(b) The propositional image can be rewritten as the finite program

$$p(5), \ p(6), \ p(7),$$
$$q(n) \leftarrow \neg p(n) \qquad (n = 1, \ldots, 5),$$

and transformed, using Theorem on Irrelevant Formulas and Theorem on Facts, into the set of atoms

$$p(5), \ p(6), \ p(7), \ q(1), \ q(2), \ q(3), \ q(4).$$

These atoms form the only stable model of the given program.

5.11.

(a)

$$p(5) \wedge p(6) \wedge p(7),$$
$$q(n) \leftarrow p(n) \wedge \neg p(m) \qquad \text{for all integers } n,$$
$$\text{where } m \text{ is the value of } n + 1,$$
$$q(v) \leftarrow p(v) \wedge \top \qquad \text{for all symbolic constants } v.$$

(b) Using Theorem on Irrelevant Formulas, we can rewrite the propositional image as

$$p(5), \ p(6), \ p(7),$$
$$q(5) \leftarrow p(5) \wedge \neg p(6),$$
$$q(6) \leftarrow p(6) \wedge \neg p(7),$$
$$q(7) \leftarrow p(7).$$

Then Theorem on Facts allows us to transform it into its stable model

$$\{p(5), p(6), p(7), q(7)\}.$$

5.12. (a) Consider an arbitrary interpretation I. Case 1: $p \in I$. Then the reduct of the program relative to I is

$$p \vee q,$$
$$\bot \vee r.$$

The second rule is equivalent to r. The minimal models of the reduct are $\{p, r\}$ and $\{q, r\}$. Consequently $\{p, r\}$ is a stable model of the program. Case 2: $p \notin I$. Then the reduct is

$$p \vee q,$$
$$\top \vee r.$$

The second rule is a tautology. The minimal models of the reduct are $\{p\}$ and $\{q\}$. Consequently $\{q\}$ is another stable model.

5.14.

(a)

$$p(a),$$
$$q(v) \vee \neg q(v) \leftarrow p(v) \qquad (v \in \mathbf{S} \cup \mathbf{Z}).$$

(b) By Theorem on Irrelevant Formulas, the rules in the second line with v different from a can be dropped. To find the stable models of the remaining rules

$$p(a),$$
$$q(a) \vee \neg q(a) \leftarrow p(a)$$

consider an arbitrary interpretation I. Case 1: $q(a) \in I$. The reduct is

$$p(a),$$
$$q(a) \vee \bot \leftarrow p(a).$$

The second rule is equivalent to $q(a) \leftarrow p(a)$, so that the minimal model of the reduct is $\{p(a), q(a)\}$. Case 2: $q(a) \notin I$. The reduct is

$$p(a),$$
$$q(a) \vee \top \leftarrow p(a).$$

The second rule is a tautology, so that the minimal model of the reduct is $\{p(a)\}$. Consequently the stable models of the program are $\{p(a)\}$ and $\{p(a), q(a)\}$.

5.15.

(a)

$$p(a) \vee \neg p(a),$$
$$q(v) \vee \neg q(v) \leftarrow p(v) \qquad (v \in \mathbf{S} \cup \mathbf{Z}).$$

(b) By Theorem on Irrelevant Formulas, the rules in the second line with v different from a can be dropped. To find the stable models of the remaining rules

$$p(a) \vee \neg p(a),$$
$$q(a) \vee \neg q(a) \leftarrow p(a)$$

consider an arbitrary interpretation I. Case 1: $p(a), q(a) \in I$. The reduct is

$$p(a) \vee \bot,$$
$$q(a) \vee \bot \leftarrow p(a),$$

or, equivalently,

$$p(a),$$
$$q(a) \leftarrow p(a).$$

The minimal model $\{p(a), q(a)\}$ of the reduct is a stable model of the program. Case 2: $p(a) \in I, q(a) \notin I$. The reduct is

$$p(a) \vee \bot,$$
$$q(a) \vee \top \leftarrow p(a),$$

which is equivalent to $p(a)$. Interpretation $\{p(a)\}$ is a stable model. Case 3: $p(a) \notin I, q(a) \in I$. The reduct is

$$p(a) \vee \top,$$
$$q(a) \vee \bot \leftarrow p(a),$$

which is equivalent to $q(a) \leftarrow p(a)$. The minimal model $\emptyset$ of the reduct does not satisfy the conditions characterizing this case. Case 4: $p(a), q(a) \notin I$. The reduct is a pair of tautologies

$$p(a) \vee \top,$$
$$q(a) \vee \top \leftarrow p(a),$$

and its minimal model $\emptyset$ is the third stable model.

5.16.

(a)

$$p(0) \wedge p(1),$$
$$q(m) \vee \neg q(m) \leftarrow p(n) \qquad \text{for all } n \text{ in } \mathbf{Z} \setminus \{0\},$$
$$\text{where } m \text{ is the value of } \lfloor 5/n \rfloor,$$
$$\top \leftarrow p(v) \qquad \text{for all } v \text{ in } \mathbf{S} \cup \{0\}.$$

(b) Using Theorem on Irrelevant Formulas, we can rewrite the propositional image as

$$p(0),$$
$$p(1),$$
$$q(5) \vee \neg q(5) \leftarrow p(1).$$

By Theorem on Facts, the body of the last rule can be dropped. The stable models are $\{p(0), p(1)\}$ and $\{p(0), p(1), q(5)\}$.

5.17.

(a)

$$p(5),$$
$$(q(v, 0) \vee \neg q(v, 0)) \wedge (q(v, 1) \vee \neg q(v, 1)) \leftarrow p(v) \qquad \text{for all } v \text{ in } \mathbf{S} \cup \mathbf{Z}.$$

(b) Using Theorem on Irrelevant Formulas and Theorem on Facts, we can rewrite the propositional image as

$$p(5),$$
$$q(5, 0) \vee \neg q(5, 0),$$
$$q(5, 1) \vee \neg q(5, 1).$$

The stable models are

$$\{p(5)\}, \ \{p(5), q(5, 0)\}, \ \{p(5), q(5, 1)\}, \ \{p(5), q(5, 0), q(5, 1)\}. \qquad \text{(A.3)}$$

5.18. (a) From Exercise 4.13(b) we know that the stable models of the first three rules of the program are $\{p, r\}$ and $\{q, s\}$. The former satisfies both constraints, and the latter does not. It follows that the only stable model of the program is $\{p, r\}$.

5.19. (a) In Exercise 5.17 we found the stable models (A.3) of the rules in the first two lines. The propositional image of the constraint in the third line is

$$\bot \leftarrow \neg q(5, 0),$$

which is equivalent to $q(5, 0)$. It follows that the stable models of the program are $\{p(5), q(5, 0)\}$ and $\{p(5), q(5, 0), q(5, 1)\}$.

6.1. The stable model $\{p\}$ of the one-rule program p is not a stable model of the one-rule program $\neg\neg p$. Indeed, the reduct of $\neg\neg p$ relative to $\{p\}$ is $\top$, and $\{p\}$ is not a minimal model of $\top$.

6.2. Consider the programs

$$\begin{array}{l} q, \\ \neg q \leftarrow \neg p \end{array} \qquad \text{(A.4)}$$

and

$$\begin{array}{l} q, \\ p \leftarrow q. \end{array}$$

The stable model $\{p, q\}$ of the latter is not a stable model of the former. Indeed, the reduct of (A.4) relative to $\{p, q\}$ is

$$\begin{array}{l} q, \\ \bot \leftarrow \bot, \end{array}$$

and its only minimal model is $\{q\}$.

6.3. Consider sets Γ_1, Γ_2 of positive propositional rules that are equivalent to each other. The reduct of Γ_i relative to any interpretation is Γ_i. Consequently the reduct of Γ_1 relative to any interpretation is equivalent to the reduct of Γ_2 relative to the same interpretation.

6.4. True. Indeed, the propositional image of a ground rule of form (6.9) has the form

$$F \leftarrow \bot$$

if the set of values of t_1 is the same as the set of values of t_2, and

$$F \leftarrow \top$$

otherwise. The propositional image of (6.10) is

$$F \vee \top$$

or

$$F \vee \bot$$

depending on the same condition. In both cases, the propositional images are strongly equivalent to each other.

6.5. True. Indeed, if the reduct of (6.11) relative to some interpretation is $F' \leftarrow \top \wedge G'$ then the reduct of (6.12) relative to the same interpretation is $F' \vee \bot \leftarrow G'$; if the reduct of the former is $F' \leftarrow \bot \wedge G'$ then the reduct of the latter is $F' \vee \top \leftarrow G'$. Either way, the two reducts are equivalent to each other.

6.6. (a) False: $p \vee \neg p$ has two stable models, and the empty program has one. (b) True: the reduct of this rule relative to any interpretation is either $\bot \vee \top$ or $\top \vee \bot$, and both formulas are tautologies. (c) True: this formula is strongly equivalent to $\neg(F \wedge \neg F)$, and the reduct of this rule relative to any interpretation is $\top$. (d) True: any reduct $F' \leftarrow F' \wedge G'$ of this rule is a tautology. (e) True: any reduct $F' \vee G' \leftarrow F'$ of this rule is a tautology.

6.7.

(a) Add the rule $p \leftarrow q$ to both programs.
(b)

p	q	$p \leftarrow q$	$\neg q$	$p \leftarrow \neg q$	$(p \leftarrow q) \wedge (p \leftarrow \neg q)$
1/2	1/2	1	0	1	1

6.8.

(a)

$$p \leftrightarrow \top,$$
$$q \leftrightarrow \top,$$
$$r \leftrightarrow p \wedge \neg s,$$
$$s \leftrightarrow \bot.$$

(b) The result of simplifying the completion is

$$p,$$
$$q,$$
$$r \leftrightarrow \neg s,$$
$$s \leftrightarrow \bot,$$

so that $\{p, q, r\}$ is the only model of completion.

6.9. Yes: assign rank 0 to p and t, rank 1 to r, and rank 2 to q and s.

6.10.

(a) The completion of the program is

$$p \leftrightarrow \neg q,$$
$$q \leftrightarrow \neg r,$$
$$r \leftrightarrow \bot,$$

and it can be equivalently rewritten as $\{\neg p, q, \neg r\}$. The only model of completion, and consequently the only stable model of the program, is $\{q\}$.

(b) The completion of the program is

$$p \leftrightarrow \neg q,$$
$$q \leftrightarrow \neg r,$$
$$r \leftrightarrow \neg p.$$

Using the first line, we can rewrite the third line as

$$r \leftrightarrow \neg \neg q.$$

This formula can be rewritten as $r \leftrightarrow q$, which contradicts the second line. Consequently the completion of this program has no models, and the program has no stable models.

6.11. The completion of the program is

$$p \leftrightarrow \neg q \vee q,$$
$$q \leftrightarrow \neg p \vee p.$$

The first formula is equivalent to p, and the second is equivalent to q. Consequently the only model of completion is $\{p, q\}$. Since the program does not satisfy condition (γ), we need to check whether this model is stable. The reduct of the program relative to $\{p, q\}$ is

$$p \leftarrow \bot,$$
$$q \leftarrow \bot,$$
$$p \leftarrow q,$$
$$q \leftarrow p,$$

which is equivalent to $p \leftrightarrow q$. The interpretation $\{p, q\}$ is not a minimal model of $p \leftrightarrow q$. Consequently it is not a stable model of the program, so that the program has no stable models.

6.12. The simplified propositional image (5.15) of the program satisfies conditions (α)–(γ), and its completion is

$$composite(4) \leftrightarrow \top,$$
$$composite(v) \leftrightarrow \bot \qquad \text{for all } v \text{ other than 4,}$$
$$prime(v) \leftrightarrow \neg composite(v) \qquad \text{if } v \in \{2, \ldots, 5\},$$
$$prime(v) \leftrightarrow \bot \qquad \text{if } v \notin \{2, \ldots, 5\}.$$

The first two lines allow us to rewrite the last two lines as

$$prime(v) \leftrightarrow \top \qquad \text{if } v \in \{2, 3, 5\},$$
$$prime(v) \leftrightarrow \bot \qquad \text{if } v \notin \{2, 3, 5\}.$$

Consequently the only stable model of the program is

$$\{composite(4), prime(2), prime(3), prime(5)\}.$$

7.1. `:- #count{I : I = 1..n, in(I)} != m.`

7.2. `howmany(I,N) :- N = #count{C : where(C,I)}, I = 1..k.`

7.3.

(a) `large(C) :- size(C,S),`
`            #count{C1 : size(C1,S1), S1 > S} < k.`

(b)

`    large(C) :- size(C,S), #count{C1 : size(C1,S1)} = N,`
`                #count{C1 : size(C1,S1), S1 < S} >= N/2.`

7.5. `#count{X : p(X)}.`

7.6.
Line 14: `:- #sum{X : filled(R,_,X)} != magic, R = 1..n.`
Line 17: `:- #sum{X : filled(_,C,X)} != magic, C = 1..n.`
Line 20: `:- #sum{X : filled(R,R,X)} != magic.`
Line 21: `:- #sum{X : filled(R,n+1-R,X)} != magic.`

7.7. Since CLINGO does not know about fractions, we represent a score by the number of points times two.

`ranked_higher(C1,C2,N,R) :- p(R,Pos1,C1), p(R,Pos2,C2),`
`                            Pos1 < Pos2,`
`                            votecount(R,N).`
`% achieved: ranked_higher(C1,C2,N) iff C1 was ranked`
`%           higher than C2 by N voters.`

```
full_points(C,N)  :- C = 1..m, N = #count{CC :
                                    ranked_higher(C,CC,A),
                                    ranked_higher(CC,C,B),
                                    A > B, C2 = 1..m}.
% achieved: full_points(C,N) iff C earned one point
                                    in N competitions.


half_points(C,N)  :- C = 1..m, N = #count{CC :
                                    ranked_higher(C,CC,A),
                                    ranked_higher(CC,C,A),
             C != CC, CC = 1..m}.
% achieved: half_points(C,N) iff C earned a half-point
%              in N competitions.


score(C,2*N1+N2)  :- full_points(C,N1),
                     half_points(C,N2).
% achieved: score(C,N) iff N equals 2 times the total
%              number of points earned by C.


loser(C)  :- score(C,N), score(C1,N1), N1 > N.
% achieved: loser(C) iff candidate C earned fewer
%              points than another candidate.


winner(C)  :- C = 1..m, not loser(C).
% achieved: winner(C) iff C is a winner.


#show winner/1.
```

7.8. (a):- #count$\{I : p(I)\}$ = 0. (b):- #max$\{X : p(X)\}$ = #inf.
(c):- #min$\{X : p(X)\}$ = #sup.

7.9.

```
howmany(I,N)  :- N = #count{C : where(C,I)}, I = 1..K,
              K = #max{J : where(C,J)}.
```

7.10. Add the rule :- #sum$\{Vol,I : in(I),$ volume$(I,Vol)\}$
                                                        > maxvolume.

7.11.
Line 10: $\{in(I,0..maxweight/W)\}$ = 1 :- weight(I,W).
Line 15: :- #sum$\{W*N,I : in(I,N),$ weight$(I,W)\}$ > maxweight.
Line 20: #maximize$\{V*N,I : in(I,N),$ value$(I,V)\}$.

7.12. #maximize$\{1,I : in(I)\}$.

7.13. Line 6: `{in(X)} :- vertex(X).`
Line 13: `#maximize{1,I : in(I)}.`

7.14.
Line 7: `referee(R) :- bid(R,_,_).`
Line 11: `paper(P) :- bid(_,P,_).`
Line 17: `{review(R,P) : referee(R), not bid(R,P,no)} = k :-`
                                                        `paper(P).`
Line 22: `workload(R,N) :- referee(R),`
                        `N = #count{P : review(R,P)}.`
Line 26: `:- workload(R1,N1), workload(R2,N2), |N1-N2| > 1.`
Line 31: `#maximize{1,R,P : bid(R,P,yes), review(R,P)}.`

7.15. `f(1,g(1)), f(1,g(2)), f(2,g(1)), f(2,g(2)).`

8.1. (a) $n(n-1)$. (b) n^2. (c) $n^2 - n + m$.

8.2. Initial state S_1; goal S_3.

8.3. (a) 30. (b) 3. (c) 4.

8.4.

$$(loaded, alive) \qquad\qquad (loaded, dead)$$

$$load \uparrow \quad\ shoot \searrow \quad shoot \downarrow \uparrow load$$

$$(unloaded, alive) \qquad (unloaded, dead)$$

8.5. Self-loops at the vertices (*unloaded, alive*) and (*unloaded, dead*) will be added, labeled *shoot*.

8.6. (a)

$$pull(1)$$

$$0 \longrightarrow 1$$

$$pull(1) \uparrow \qquad\qquad \downarrow pull(1)$$

$$3 \longleftarrow 2$$

$$pull(1)$$

(b) $n4^n$. (c) Edge labeled *pull*(1) leading to (1,0,3); edge labeled *pull*(2) leading to (0,1,3); edge labeled *pull*(3) leading to (0,0,0).

8.7. (a) $2n - 1$. (b) $2n + 1$.

8.8.

```
#const h=2.
holds(state_of_gun(unloaded),0).
holds(state_of_turkey(alive),0).
occurs(load,0).
occurs(shoot,1).
```

8.9.

```
#const h=1.
holds(brightness(bulb(1),0),0).
holds(brightness(bulb(2),0),0).
holds(brightness(bulb(3),3),0).
occurs(pull(3),0).
```

8.10.

```
#const h=4.
holds(loc(a,left),0).
holds(loc(b,left),0).
holds(loc(boat,right),0).
occurs(cross(empty),0).
occurs(cross(a),1).
occurs(cross(empty),2).
occurs(cross(b),3).
```

8.11.

(a)

```
:- #count{S : holds(state_of_gun(S),T)} != 1,
                                          T = 0..h.
:- #count{S : holds(state_of_turkey(S),T)} != 1,
                                          T = 0..h.
```

(b)
```
:- #count{B : holds(brightness(bulb(I),B),T)} != 1,
                                    I = 1..n, T = 0..h.
```

(c)

```
:- #count{L : holds(loc(I,L),T)} != 1, item(I),
:- #count{L : holds(loc(boat,L),T)} != 1, T = 0..h.
```

8.12.

```
holds(brightness(bulb(I),(B+1)\4),T+1) :-
        occurs(pull(I),T),
        holds(brightness (bulb(I),B),T).
```

8.13.

(a)

```
holds(state_of_gun(X),T+1) :-
                holds(state_of_gun(X),T),
                not not holds(state_of_gun(X),T+1),
                T = 0..h-1.
holds(state_of_turkey(X),T+1) :-
                holds(state_of_turkey(X),T),
                not not holds(state_of_turkey(X),T+1),
                T = 0..h-1.
```

(b)

```
holds(brightness(bulb(I),B),T+1) :-
        holds(brightness(bulb(I),B),T),
        not not holds(brightness(bulb(I),B),T+1),
        T = 0..h-1.
```

(c) Rule (8.9) will do.

8.14.

```
{holds(brightness(bulb(I),B),T+1)} :-
                holds(brightness(bulb(I),B),T),
                T = 0..h-1.
```

8.15. After this change, table will become a possible value of B.

8.16. :- occurs(move(_,B),T), holds(loc(_,B),T), block(B).

8.17.

```
:- occurs(shoot,T), holds(state_of_gun(unloaded),T).
:- occurs(load,T), holds(state_of_gun(loaded),T).
```

8.18.

```
L1 = L2 :- occurs(cross(I),T), item(I),
           holds(loc(I,L1),T), holds(loc(boat,L2),T).
```

8.19. (a)

```
% Predict the effect of executing a sequence of
% actions in the turkey shoot domain.

% input: length h of the sequence of actions; set
%         init/1 of atoms representing the initial
%         state; set occurs/2 of pairs (a,t) such that
%         action a is executed between times t and t+1.

% effects of actions
holds(state_of_gun(loaded),T+1) :- occurs(load,T).
holds(state_of_gun(unloaded),T+1) :- occurs(shoot,T).
holds(state_of_turkey(dead),T+1) :- occurs(shoot,T).

% loading is impossible if the gun is loaded
:- occurs(load,T), holds(state_of_gun(loaded),T).

% shooting is impossible if the gun is unloaded
:- occurs(shoot,T), holds(state_of_gun(unloaded),T).

% existence and uniqueness of value
:- #count{X : holds(state_of_gun(X),T)} != 1,
                                        T = 0..h.
:- #count{X : holds(state_of_turkey(X),T)} != 1,
                                        T = 0..h.

% inertia
{holds(state_of_gun(X),T+1)} :-
              holds(state_of_gun(X),T), T = 0..h-1.
{holds(state_of_turkey(X),T+1)} :-
              holds(state_of_turkey(X),T), T = 0..h-1.

% Relationship between holds/2, init/1, and final/1
holds(C,0) :- init(C).
final(C) :- holds(C,h).

#show final/1.
```

(b)

```
#const h=3.
init(state_of_gun(unloaded); state_of_turkey(alive)).
occurs(load,0; shoot,1; load,2).
```

8.20. (a)

```
% Predict the effect of executing a sequence of
%   actions in the 3-way bulb domain.

% input: number n of bulbs; length h of the sequence
%          of actions; set init/1 of atoms representing
%          the initial state; set occurs/2 of pairs
%          (a,t) such that action a is executed between
%          times t and t+1.

% effects of actions
holds(brightness(bulb(I),(B+1)\4),T+1)  :-
              occurs(pull(I),T),
              holds(brightness(bulb(I),B),T).

% existence and uniqueness of value
:- #count{B : holds(brightness(bulb(I),B),T)} != 1,
                            I = 1..n, T = 0..h.

% inertia
{holds(brightness(bulb(I),B),T+1)}  :- holds(brightness
                                    (bulb(I),B),T),
                                    T = 0..h-1.

% relationship between holds/2, init/1, and final/1
holds(C,0)  :- init(C).
final(C)  :- holds(C,h).

#show final/1.
```

(b)

```
#const n=10.
#const h=10.
init(brightness(bulb(1..10),3)).
occurs(pull(I),I-1)  :- I = 1..10.
```

8.21. (a)

```
% Predict the effect of executing a sequence of
%   actions in the crossing the river domain.

% input: set item/1 of items; length h of the sequence
%         of actions; set init/1 of atoms representing
%         the initial state; set occurs/2 of pairs
%         (a,t) such that action a is executed between
%         times t and t+1.

% definition of opposite/2.
opposite(left,right; right,left).

% effects of actions
holds(loc(boat,L1),T+1)  :- occurs(cross(_),T),
                            holds(loc(boat,L),T),
                            opposite(L,L1).
holds(loc(I,L1),T+1)  :- occurs(cross(I),T), item(I),
                         holds(loc(I,L),T),
                         opposite(L,L1).

% existence and uniqueness of value
:- #count{L : holds(loc(I,L),T)} != 1, item(I),
                                T = 0..h.
:- #count{L : holds(loc(boat,L),T)} != 1,
                                T = 0..h.

% inertia
{holds(loc(X,L),T+1)} :- holds(loc(X,L),T),
                              T = 0..h-1.

% relationship between holds/2, init/1, and final/1
holds(C,0) :- init(C).
final(C) :- holds(C,h).

#show final/1.
```

(b)

```
item(a; b).
#const h=1.
init(loc(a,left); loc(boat,left); loc(b,right)).
occurs(cross(a),0).
```

8.24. (a)

```
block(1..9).
init(loc(1,2); loc(2,3); loc(3,4); loc(4,table);
     loc(5,6); loc(6,7); loc(7,table);
     loc(8,9); loc(9,table)).
goal(loc(9,6); loc(6,3); loc(3,table)).
#const h=7.
```

8.25. (a)

```
% choice of actions
action(load; shoot).
{occurs(A,T) : action(A) } = 1 :- T = 0..h-1.

% effects of actions
holds(state_of_gun(loaded),T+1) :- occurs(load,T).
holds(state_of_gun(unloaded),T+1) :- occurs(shoot,T).
holds(state_of_turkey(dead),T+1) :- occurs(shoot,T).

% loading is impossible if the gun is loaded
:- occurs(load,T), holds(state_of_gun(loaded),T).

% shooting is impossible if the gun is unloaded
:- occurs(shoot,T), holds(state_of_gun(unloaded),T).

% existence and uniqueness of value
:- #count{X : holds(state_of_gun(X),T)} != 1,
                                        T = 0..h.
:- #count{X : holds(state_of_turkey(X),T)} != 1,
                                        T = 0..h.

% inertia
{holds(state_of_gun(X),T+1)} :-
                holds(state_of_gun(X),T),
                T = 0..h-1.
{holds(state_of_turkey(X),T+1)} :-
                holds(state_of_turkey(X),T),
                T = 0..h-1.

% relationship between holds/2, init/1, and goal/1.
holds(C,0) :- init(C).
:- goal(C), not holds(C,h).

#show occurs/2.
```

8.26. (a)

```
% choice of actions
action(pull(1..n)).
{occurs(A,T) : action(A) } = 1 :- T = 0..h-1.

% effects of actions
holds(brightness(bulb(I),(B+1)\4),T+1) :-
    occurs(pull(I),T), holds(brightness(bulb(I),B),T).

% existence and uniqueness of value
:- #count{B : holds(brightness(bulb(I),B),T)} != 1,
                                    I = 1..n, T = 0..h.

% inertia
{holds(brightness(bulb(I),B),T+1)}:-
                holds(brightness(bulb(I),B),T),
                T = 0..h-1.

% relationship between holds/2, init/1, and goal/1.
holds(C,0) :- init(C).
:- goal(C), not holds(C,h).

#show occurs/2.
```

8.28. (a)

```
% choice of actions
action(cross(I)) :- item(I).
action(cross(empty)).
{occurs(A,T) : action(A) } = 1 :- T = 0..h-1.

% definition of opposite/2.
  opposite(left,right; right,left).

% effects of actions
  holds(loc(boat,L1),T+1) :- occurs(cross(_),T),
                            holds(loc(boat,L),T),
                            opposite(L,L1).
  holds(loc(I,L1),T+1) :- occurs(cross(I),T), item(I),
                            holds(loc(I,L),T),
                            opposite(L,L1).

% existence and uniqueness of value
:- #count{L : holds(loc(I,L),T)} != 1,item(I),T =0..h.
:- #count{L : holds(loc(boat,L),T)} != 1, T = 0..h.
```

```
% inertia
{holds(loc(X,L),T+1)} :- holds(loc(X,L),T),T = 0..h-1.

% relationship between holds/2, init/1, and goal/1.
holds(C,0) :- init(C).
:- goal(C), not holds(C,h).

#show occurs/2.
```

(b)

```
item(fox; goose; beans).

init(loc(boat,left)).
init(loc(I,left)) :- item(I).

goal(loc(boat,right)).
goal(loc(I,right)) :- item(I).

:- holds(loc(fox,L),T), holds(loc(goose,L),T),
                        not holds(loc(boat,L),T).
:- holds(loc(goose,L),T), holds(loc(beans,L),T),
                        not holds(loc(boat,L),T).

#const h=10.

action(wait).
#maximize{T : occurs(wait,T)}.
```

8.29.

```
#const size=4.

loc((1..size,1..size)).

% choice of actions
action(move(L1,L2)) :- loc(L1), loc(L2).
action(wait).
{occurs(A,T) : action(A)} = 1 :- T = 0..h-1.

% effects of actions
holds(loc(N,L2),T+1) :- occurs(move(L1,L2),T),
                        holds(loc(N,L1),T).
```

```
|R1-R2|+|C1-C2| = 1 :- occurs(move((R1,C1),
                                    (R2,C2))),T).
:- occurs(move(_,L),T), holds(loc(N,L),T).

% existence and uniqueness of value
:- #count{L : holds(loc(N,L),T)} != 1, N=1..size**2-1,
                                              T=0..h.

% inertia
{holds(loc(N,L),T+1)} :- holds(loc(N,L),T),T = 0..h-1.

% relationship between holds/2, init/1, and goal/1.
holds(loc(N,(R,C)),0) :- init(R,C,N).
:- goal(R,C,N), not holds(loc(N,(R,C)),h).

#show occurs/2.
```

8.30.

```
% input: the number n of disks.

#const h=2**n-1.
peg(a; b; c).
disk(1..n).
holds(loc(D,a),0) :- disk(D).
:- not holds(loc(D,c),h), disk(D).

% choice of actions
action(move(D,P)) :- disk(D), peg(P).
{occurs(A,T) : action(A)} = 1 :- T = 0..h-1.

% effects of actions
holds(loc(D,P),T+1) :- occurs(move(D,P),T).

:- occurs(move(D,P),T), holds(loc(D,P),T).

:- occurs(move(D,P),T), holds(loc(D1,P),T), D1 > D.

:- occurs(move(D,P),T), holds(loc(D,P1),T),
   holds(loc(D1,P1),T), D1 > D.

% existence and uniqueness of value
:- #count{P : holds(loc(D,P),T)} != 1, disk(D),
                                        T = 0..h.
```

```
% inertia
{holds(loc(D,P),T+1)}  :- holds(loc(D,P),T),
                                    T = 0..h-1.

#show occurs/2.
```

8.32. (a) Replace the line

```
{occurs(A,T)  :  action(A)  } = 1 :- T = 0..h-1.
```

by

```
1 {occurs(A,T)  :  action(A)  } 2 :- T = 0..h-1.
```

Listings

© Springer Nature Switzerland AG 2019
V. Lifschitz, *Answer Set Programming*,
https://doi.org/10.1007/978-3-030-24658-7

Bibliography

1. *AI Magazine*, 37(3), 2016. Special Issue on Answer Set Programming.
2. *Artificial Intelligence*, 13(1,2), 1980.
3. Markus Aschinger, Conrad Drescher, Gerhard Friedrich, Georg Gottlob, Peter Jeavons, Anna Ryabokon, and Evgenij Thorstensen. Optimization methods for the partner units problem. In *Proceedings of the Eigth International Conference on Integration of AI and OR Techniques in Constraint Programming for Combinatorial Optimization Problems*, pages 4–19, 2011.
4. Evgenii Balai, Michael Gelfond, and Yuanlin Zhang. Towards Answer Set Programming with sorts. In *Proceedings of the Twelfth International Conference on Logic Programming and Nonmonotonic Reasoning*, pages 135–147, 2013.
5. Marcello Balduccini. CR-models: an inference engine for CR-Prolog. In *Proceedings of the Eighteenth International Conference on Logic Programming and Nonmonotonic Reasoning*, pages 18–30, 2005.
6. Marcello Balduccini. ASP with non-Herbrand partial functions: a language and system for practical use. *Theory and Practice of Logic Programming*, 13:547–561, 2013.
7. Marcello Balduccini and Michael Gelfond. Logic programs with consistency-restoring rules. In *Working Notes of the AAAI Spring Symposium on Logical Formalizations of Commonsense Reasoning*, 2003.
8. Marcello Balduccini and Yuliya Lierler. Constraint answer set solver EZCSP and why integration schemas matter. *Theory and Practice of Logic Programming*, 17:462–515, 2017.
9. Mutsunori Banbara, Benjamin Kaufmann, Max Ostrowski, and Torsten Schaub. Clingcon: The next generation. *Theory and Practice of Logic Programming*, 17:408–461, 2017.
10. Chitta Baral. *Knowledge Representation, Reasoning and Declarative Problem Solving*. Cambridge University Press, 2003.
11. Michael Bartholomew and Joohyung Lee. Stable models of formulas with intensional functions. In *Proceedings of International Conference on Principles of Knowledge Representation and Reasoning*, pages 2–12, 2012.
12. Leonard Baumert and Solomon Golomb. Backtrack programming. *Journal of the ACM*, 12:516–524, 1965.
13. Nicole Bidoit and Christine Froidevaux. Minimalism subsumes default logic and circumscription in stratified logic programming. In *Proceedings of the Second Annual IEEE Symposium on Logic in Computer Science*, pages 89–97, 1987.
14. Gerhard Brewka. Logic programming with ordered disjunction. In *Proceedings of the Eighteenth National Conference on Artificial Intelligence*, pages 100–105, 2003.
15. Gerhard Brewka, James Delgrande, Javier Romero, and Torsten Schaub. asprin: Customizing answer set preferences without a headache. In *Proceedings of the Twenty-Ninth AAAI Conference on Artificial Intelligence*, pages 1467–1474, 2015.

© Springer Nature Switzerland AG 2019
V. Lifschitz, *Answer Set Programming*,
https://doi.org/10.1007/978-3-030-24658-7

16. Luitzen Egbertus Jan Brouwer. Über die Bedeutung des Satzes vom ausgeschlossenen Dritten in der Mathematik, insbesondere in der Funktiontheorie. *Journal für die reine und angewandte Mathematik*, 154:1–7, 1923.

17. Pedro Cabalar. Functional Answer Set Programming. *Theory and Practice of Logic Programming*, 11:203–234, 2011.

18. Marco Calautti, Sergio Greco, and Irina Trubitsyna. Detecting decidable classes of finitely ground logic programs with function symbols. *ACM Transactions on Computational Logic*, 18(4):28:1–28:42, November 2017.

19. Francesco Calimeri, Susanna Cozza, Giovambattista Ianni, and Nicola Leone. Computable functions in ASP: theory and implementation. In *Proceedings of International Conference on Logic Programming (ICLP)*, pages 407–424, 2008.

20. Günther Charwat and Andreas Pfandler. Democratix: A declarative approach to winner determination. In *Proceedings of the 4th International Conference on Algorithmic Decision Theory (ADT)*, 2015.

21. Baral Chitta, Michael Gelfond, and Nelson Rushton. Probabilistic reasoning with answer sets. *Theory and Practice of Logic Programming*, 9:57–144, 2009.

22. Pawel Cholewiński, Victor Marek, and Miroslaw Truszczynski. Default reasoning system DeReS. In *Proceedings of International Conference on Principles of Knowledge Representation and Reasoning (KR)*, pages 518–528, 1996.

23. Vašek Chvátal. Some unknown van der Waerden numbers. In Richard Guy, Haim Hanani, and Norbert Sauer, editors, *Combinatorial Structures and Their Applications*, pages 31–33. New York: Gordon and Breach, 2009.

24. Simona Citrigno, Thomas Eiter, Wolfgang Faber, Georg Gottlob, Christoph Koch, Leone Nicola, Cristinel Mateis, Gerald Pfeifer, and Francesco Scarcello. The DLV system: Model generator and application frontends. In *Proceedings of Workshop on Logic Programming (WLP97)*, 1997.

25. Keith Clark. Negation as failure. In Herve Gallaire and Jack Minker, editors, *Logic and Data Bases*, pages 293–322. Plenum Press, New York, 1978.

26. Stephen A. Cook. The complexity of theorem-proving procedures. In *Proceedings Third Annual ACM Symposium on Theory of Computing*, 1971.

27. Martin Davis, George Logemann, and Donald Loveland. A machine program for theorem proving. *Communications of the ACM*, 5(7):394–397, 1962.

28. Yannis Dimopoulos, Bernhard Nebel, and Jana Koehler. Encoding planning problems in non-monotonic logic programs. In Sam Steel and Rachid Alami, editors, *Proceedings of European Conference on Planning*, pages 169–181. Springer, 1997.

29. Thomas Eiter, Michael Fink, Giovambattista Ianni, Thomas Krennwallner, Christoph Redl, and Peter Schüller. A model building framework for Answer Set Programming with external computations. *Theory and Practice of Logic Programming*, 16(4):418–464, 2016.

30. Thomas Eiter, Nicola Leone, Cristinel Mateis, Gerald Pfeifer, and Francesco Scarcello. The KR system DLV: Progress report, comparisons and benchmarks. In Anthony Cohn, Lenhart Schubert, and Stuart Shapiro, editors, *Proceedings of International Conference on Principles of Knowledge Representation and Reasoning (KR)*, pages 406–417, 1998.

31. Esra Erdem, Michael Gelfond, and Nicola Leone. Applications of Answer Set Programming. *AI Magazine*, 37:53–68, 2016.

32. Esra Erdem and Vladimir Lifschitz. Fages' theorem for programs with nested expressions. In *Proceedings of International Conference on Logic Programming (ICLP)*, pages 242–254, 2001.

33. Esra Erdem and Vladimir Lifschitz. Tight logic programs. *Theory and Practice of Logic Programming*, 3:499–518, 2003.

34. Wolfgang Faber, Gerald Pfeifer, and Nicola Leone. Semantics and complexity of recursive aggregates in Answer Set Programming. *Artificial Intelligence*, 175:278–298, 2011.

35. François Fages. Consistency of Clark's completion and existence of stable models. *Journal of Methods of Logic in Computer Science*, 1:51–60, 1994.

36. Andreas Falkner, Gerhard Friedrich, Konstantin Schekotihin, Richard Taupe, and Erich Teppan. Industrial applications of Answer Set Programming. *Künstliche Intelligenz*, 32:165–176, 2018.

37. Paolo Ferraris. Answer sets for propositional theories. In *Proceedings of International Conference on Logic Programming and Nonmonotonic Reasoning (LPNMR)*, pages 119–131, 2005.

38. Paolo Ferraris and Vladimir Lifschitz. Weight constraints as nested expressions. *Theory and Practice of Logic Programming*, 5(1–2):45–74, 2005.

39. Richard Fikes and Nils Nilsson. STRIPS: A new approach to the application of theorem proving to problem solving. *Artificial Intelligence*, 2(3–4):189–208, 1971.

40. Kit Fine. The justification of negation as failure. In *Proceedings of the Eighth International Congress of Logic, Methodology and Philosophy of Science*, pages 263–301. North Holland, 1989.

41. Raphael Finkel, Wiktor Marek, and Miroslaw Truszczynski. Constraint Lingo: towards high-level constraint programming. *Software: Practice and Experience*, 34(15):1481–1504, 2004.

42. John Franco and John Martin. A history of satisfiability. In Armin Biere, Marijn Heule, Hans van Maaren, and Toby Walsh, editors, *Handbook of Satisfiability*, pages 7–74. IOS Press, 2009.

43. Harold Fredricksen and Melvin Sweet. Symmetric sum-free partitions and lower bounds for Schur numbers. *Electronic Journal of Combinatorics*, 7, 2000.

44. Martin Gebser, Amelia Harrison, Roland Kaminski, Vladimir Lifschitz, and Torsten Schaub. Abstract gringo. *Theory and Practice of Logic Programming*, 15:449–463, 2015.

45. Martin Gebser, Roland Kaminski, Benjamin Kaufmann, and Torsten Schaub. *Answer Set Solving in Practice*. Synthesis Lectures on Artificial Intelligence and Machine Learning. Morgan and Claypool Publishers, 2012.

46. Martin Gebser, Marco Maratea, and Francesco Ricca. The design of the seventh Answer Set Programming competition. In *Proceedings of the Fourteenth International Conference on Logic Programming and Nonmonotonic Reasoning*, pages 3–9. Springer, 2017.

47. Martin Gebser, Max Ostrowski, and Torsten Schaub. Constraint answer set solving. In *Proceedings of 25th International Conference on Logic Programming (ICLP)*, pages 235–249. Springer, 2009.

48. Michael Gelfond. On stratified autoepistemic theories. In *Proceedings of National Conference on Artificial Intelligence (AAAI)*, pages 207–211, 1987.

49. Michael Gelfond. Answer sets. In Frank van Harmelen, Vladimir Lifschitz, and Bruce Porter, editors, *Handbook of Knowledge Representation*, pages 285–316. Elsevier, 2008.

50. Michael Gelfond and Yulia Kahl. *Knowledge Representation, Reasoning, and the Design of Intelligent Agents: The Answer-Set Programming Approach*. Cambridge University Press, 2014.

51. Michael Gelfond and Vladimir Lifschitz. The stable model semantics for logic programming. In Robert Kowalski and Kenneth Bowen, editors, *Proceedings of International Logic Programming Conference and Symposium*, pages 1070–1080. MIT Press, 1988.

52. Michael Gelfond and Vladimir Lifschitz. Logic programs with classical negation. In David Warren and Peter Szeredi, editors, *Proceedings of International Conference on Logic Programming (ICLP)*, pages 579–597, 1990.

53. Michael Gelfond and Vladimir Lifschitz. Classical negation in logic programs and disjunctive databases. *New Generation Computing*, 9:365–385, 1991.

54. Michael Gelfond and Vladimir Lifschitz. Representing actions in extended logic programming. In Krzysztof Apt, editor, *Proceedings Joint International Conference and Symp. on Logic Programming*, pages 559–573, 1992.

55. Michael Gelfond and Yuanlin Zhang. Vicious circle principle and logic programs with aggregates. *Theory and Practice of Logic Programming*, 14(4-5):587–601, 2014.

56. Malik Ghallab, Dana Nau, and Paolo Traverso. *Automated planning and acting*. Cambridge University Press, 2016.

57. Herman Goldstine. *The computer from Pascal to von Neumann*. Princeton University Press, 1973.
58. Carla Gomes, Henry Kautz, Ashish Sabharwal, and Bart Selman. Satisfiability solvers. In Frank van Harmelen, Vladimir Lifschitz, and Bruce Porter, editors, *Handbook of Knowledge Representation*, pages 89–134. Elsevier, 2008.
59. Cordell Green. Application of theorem proving to problem solving.
    In *Proceedings of International Joint Conference on Artificial Intelligence (IJCAI)*, pages 219–240, 1969.
60. Steve Hanks and Drew McDermott.
    Default reasoning, nonmonotonic logics, and the frame problem. In *Proceedings of National Conference on Artificial Intelligence (AAAI)*, 1986.
61. Steve Hanks and Drew McDermott. Nonmonotonic logic and temporal projection. *Artificial Intelligence*, 33(3):379–412, 1987.
62. W.L. Harper, G.A. Pearce, and R. Stalnaker, editors. *IFS: Conditionals, Belief, Decision, Chance and Time*. Springer, 1980.
63. Amelia Harrison and Vladimir Lifschitz. Relating two dialects of Answer Set Programming. In *Proceedings of International Conference on Logic Programming (ICLP)*, 2019.
64. Amelia Harrison, Vladimir Lifschitz, and Fangkai Yang. The semantics of Gringo and infinitary propositional formulas. In *Proceedings of International Conference on Principles of Knowledge Representation and Reasoning (KR)*, 2014.
65. Marijn Heule. Schur number five. In *Proceedings of AAAI Conference on Artificial Intelligence*, 2018.
66. Arend Heyting. Die formalen Regeln der intuitionistischen Logik. *Sitzungsberichte der Preussischen Akademie von Wissenschaften. Physikalisch-mathematische Klasse*, pages 42–56, 1930.
67. Tomi Janhunen, Roland Kaminski, Max Ostrowski, Sebastian Schellhorn, Philipp Wanko, and Torsten Schaub. Clingo goes linear constraints over reals and integers. *Theory and Practice of Logic Programming*, 17:872–888, 2017.
68. Carol Ruth Karp. *Languages with expressions of infinite length*. North-Holland, Amsterdam, 1964.
69. Richard Karp. Reducibility among combinatorial problems. In R. E. Miller and J. W. Thatcher, editors, *Complexity of Computer Computations*, pages 85–103. Plenum, 1972.
70. Henry Kautz and Bart Selman. Planning as satisfiability. In *Proceedings of European Conference on Artificial Intelligence (ECAI)*, pages 359–363, 1992.
71. Daniel Korman, Erik Mack, Jacob Jett, and Allen Renear. Defining textual entailment. *Journal of the Association for Information Science and Technology*, 69(6):763–772, 2018.
72. Michal Kouril. Computing the van der Waerden number W(3,4)=293. *Integers*, 2012.
73. Robert Kowalski. The early years of logic programming. *Communications of the ACM*, 31(1), 1988.
74. Gottfried Wilhelm Leibniz. *Philosophical Writings*. Everyman, 1995.
75. Nicola Leone, Gerald Pfeifer, Wolfgang Faber, Thomas Eiter, Georg Gottlob, Simona Perri, and Francesco Scarcello. The DLV system for knowledge representation and reasoning. *ACM Transactions on Computational Logic*, 7(3):499–562, 2006.
76. Yuliya Lierler. *SAT-Based Answer Set Programming*. PhD thesis, University of Texas at Austin, 2010.
77. Yuliya Lierler and Vladimir Lifschitz. One more decidable class of finitely ground programs. In *Proceedings of International Conference on Logic Programming (ICLP)*, 2009.
78. Yuliya Lierler and Vladimir Lifschitz. Termination of grounding is not preserved by strongly equivalent transformations. In *Procedings of International Conference on Logic Programming and Nonmonotonic Reasoning (LPNMR)*, 2011.
79. Vladimir Lifschitz. Thirteen definitions of a stable model. In *Fields of Logic and Computation: Essays Dedicated to Yuri Gurevich on the Occasion of his 70th Birthday*, pages 488–503. Springer, 2010.

80. Vladimir Lifschitz. The dramatic true story of the frame default. *Journal of Philosophical Logic*, 44(2):163–176, 2015.
81. Vladimir Lifschitz. Intelligent instantiation and supersafe rules. In *Technical Communications of the 28th International Conference on Logic Programming (ICLP)*, 2016.
82. Vladimir Lifschitz, David Pearce, and Agustin Valverde. Strongly equivalent logic programs. *ACM Transactions on Computational Logic*, 2:526–541, 2001.
83. Vladimir Lifschitz, Lappoon R. Tang, and Hudson Turner. Nested expressions in logic programs. *Annals of Mathematics and Artificial Intelligence*, 25:369–389, 1999.
84. Vladimir Lifschitz and Hudson Turner. Splitting a logic program. In Pascal Van Hentenryck, editor, *Proceedings of International Conference on Logic Programming (ICLP)*, pages 23–37, 1994.
85. Fangzhen Lin and Yuting Zhao. ASSAT: Computing answer sets of a logic program by SAT solvers. *Artificial Intelligence*, 157:115–137, 2004.
86. John Lloyd. *Foundations of Logic Programming*. Springer-Verlag, 1984.
87. John Lloyd and Rodney Topor. Making Prolog more expressive. *Journal of Logic Programming*, 1:225–240, 1984.
88. Jorge Lobo, Jack Minker, and Arcot Rajasekar. *Foundations of Disjunctive Logic Programming*. MIT Press, 1992.
89. Victor Marek and Miroslaw Truszczynski. Stable models and an alternative logic programming paradigm. In *The Logic Programming Paradigm: a 25-Year Perspective*, pages 375–398. Springer Verlag, 1999.
90. John McCarthy. Programs with common sense. In *Proceedings of the Teddington Conference on the Mechanization of Thought Processes*, pages 75–91, London, 1959. Reproduced in [93].
91. John McCarthy. Circumscription—a form of non-monotonic reasoning. *Artificial Intelligence*, 13:27–39,171–172, 1980.
92. John McCarthy. Applications of circumscription to formalizing common sense knowledge. *Artificial Intelligence*, 26(3):89–116, 1986.
93. John McCarthy. *Formalizing Common Sense: Papers by John McCarthy*. Ablex, Norwood, NJ, 1990.
94. John McCarthy and Patrick Hayes. Some philosophical problems from the standpoint of artificial intelligence. In B. Meltzer and D. Michie, editors, *Machine Intelligence*, volume 4, pages 463–502. Edinburgh University Press, Edinburgh, 1969.
95. Arindal Mitra and Chitta Baral. Learning to automatically solve logic grid puzzles. In *Proceedings of the 2015 Conference on Empirical Methods in Natural Language Processing*, pages 1023–1033, 2015.
96. Robert Moore. Semantical considerations on nonmonotonic logic. *Artificial Intelligence*, 25(1):75–94, 1985.
97. Ilkka Niemelä. Logic programs with stable model semantics as a constraint programming paradigm. *Annals of Mathematics and Artificial Intelligence*, 25:241–273, 1999.
98. Ilkka Niemelä and Patrik Simons. Efficient implementation of the well-founded and stable model semantics. In *Proceedings Joint International Conference and Symposium on Logic Programming*, pages 289–303, 1996.
99. Ilkka Niemelä and Patrik Simons. Extending the Smodels system with cardinality and weight constraints. In Jack Minker, editor, *Logic-Based Artificial Intelligence*, pages 491–521. Kluwer, 2000.
100. Monica Nogueira, Marcello Balduccini, Michael Gelfond, Richard Watson, and Matthew Barry. An A-Prolog decision support system for the Space Shuttle. In *Proceedings of International Symposium on Practical Aspects of Declarative Languages (PADL)*, pages 169–183, 2001.
101. David Pearce. A new logical characterization of stable models and answer sets. In Jürgen Dix, Luis Pereira, and Teodor Przymusinski, editors, *Non-Monotonic Extensions of Logic Programming (Lecture Notes in Artificial Intelligence 1216)*, pages 57–70. Springer, 1997.
102. David Pearce and Gerd Wagner. Reasoning with negative information I: Strong negation in logic programs. *Acta Philosophica Fennica*, 49, 1990.

103. Edwin Pednault. ADL: Exploring the middle ground between STRIPS and the situation calculus. In Ronald Brachman, Hector Levesque, and Raymond Reiter, editors, *Proceedings of International Conference on Principles of Knowledge Representation and Reasoning (KR)*, pages 324–332, 1989.

104. Nikolay Pelov, Marc Denecker, and Maurice Bruynooghe. Well-founded and stable semantics of logic programs with aggregates. *Theory and Practice of Logic Programming*, 7(3):301–353, 2007.

105. Emil Post. Introduction to a general theory of elementary propositions. *American Journal of Mathematics*, 43(1):163–185, 1921.

106. Raymond Reiter. On closed word data bases. In Herve Gallaire and Jack Minker, editors, *Logic and Data Bases*, pages 119–140. Plenum Press, New York, 1978.

107. Raymond Reiter. A logic for default reasoning. *Artificial Intelligence*, 13:81–132, 1980.

108. Alan Robinson. A machine-oriented logic based on the resolution principle. *Journal of ACM*, 12:23–41, 1965.

109. Issai Schur. Über die Kongruenz $x^m + y^m \equiv z^m \pmod{p}$. *Jahresbericht der Deutschen Mathematiker-Vereinigung*, 25:114–116, 1916.

110. Rolf Schwitter. The jobs puzzle: Taking on the challenge via controlled natural language processing. *Theory and Practice of Logic Programming*, 13(4,5):487–501, 2013.

111. Dana Scott and Alfred Tarski. The sentential calculus with infinitely long expressions. In *Colloquium Mathematicae*, volume 6, pages 165–170, 1958.

112. Patrik Simons. *Extending and Implementing the Stable Model Semantics*. PhD thesis, Helsinki University of Technology, 2000.

113. Tran Cao Son and Enrico Pontelli. A constructive semnatic characterization of aggregates in answer set programming. *Theory and Practice of Logic Programming*, 7:355–375, 2007.

114. Leon Sterling and Ehud Shapiro. *The Art of Prolog: Advanced Programming Techniques*. MIT Press, 1986.

115. V.S. Subrahmanian and Carlo Zaniolo. Relating stable models and AI planning domains. In *Proceedings of International Conference on Logic Programming*, pages 233–247, 1995.

116. Miroslaw Truszczynski. Connecting first-order ASP and the logic FO(ID) through reducts. In Esra Erdem, Joohyung Lee, Yuliya Lierler, and David Pearce, editors, *Correct Reasoning: Essays on Logic-Based AI in Honor of Vladimir Lifschitz*, pages 543–559. Springer, 2012.

117. Bartel Leendert van der Waerden. Beweis einer Baudetschen Vermutung. *Nieuw Archief voor Wiskunde*, 15:212–216, 1927.

118. Maarten van Emden and Keith Clark. The logic of two-person games. In *Micro-PROLOG: Programming in Logic*, pages 320–340. Prentice Hall, 1984.

119. Niklaus Wirth. *Algorithms + Data Structures = Programs*. Prentice Hall, 1976.

120. Ludwig Wittgenstein. *Tractatus Logico-philosophicus*. International library of psychology, philosophy, and scientific method. Harcourt, Brace & Company, 1922.

121. Larry Wos, Ross Overbeek, Ewing Lusk, and Jim Boyle. *Automated Reasoning: Introduction and Applications*. Prentice Hall, 1984.

Index

CPSIA information can be obtained
at www.ICGtesting.com
Printed in the USA
LVHW081935060220
646089LV00012B/324

9 783030 246570